"A groundbreaking work for the fields working with those on the spectrum, and others dealing with particular mental health challenges."

Don Waisanen, *PhD, author,* Improv for Democracy

"The approach described by the authors is quite innovative, both to watch it in action and to read about . . . Well planned and organized."

Inna Fishman, *PhD, associate clinical director, SDSU Brain Development Imaging Laboratories*

"Combining the art of improvisation along with science-based methodologies, Gary Kramer and Richie Ploesch have created a powerful, unique, and easy-to-use tool for educators and therapists. This transformative curriculum provides a fun and engaging way for neurodiverse individuals to cultivate social connections and is founded in a strengths-based approach to learning. Add this tool to your therapeutic toolbox and watch your students and clients grow in confidence and connectedness."

Sue Faber-Pew, *MA, speech-language pathologist, San Diego Unified School District*

"The world is a better place because Mr. Kramer and Mr. Ploesch have written this book. They have provided us with a way to enjoy the valuable and creative human capital of those of us with social skill challenges. Hilarity, poignancy, and health benefits are just bonuses to this awesome truth. Hurry up and play."

Les McGehee, *author,* Plays Well with Others

IMPROVISED THEATRE AND THE AUTISM SPECTRUM

This guide provides educators, professionals, and parents with an easy-to-follow and comprehensive approach to utilizing improvised theatre as a tool to teach social and communication skills to individuals on the autism spectrum.

Opening with the philosophy of the curriculum and the considerations of mental health, play, and environmental factors on individuals with autism, the book then breaks down specific activities, suggests course sequencing, and explains how each activity works and applies to desired outcomes. Packed with dozens of activities and explanations, the book includes all the information necessary to design a full curriculum or create an at-home learning program for parents.

By combining the fun and engaging atmosphere of improvisational theatre with the systematic teaching of social skills, professionals and parents can cultivate learning in a way that keeps students engaged while providing long-lasting improvements in social interaction, self-confidence, and communication.

Gary Kramer is a producer, director, and actor, and artistic director and founder of the National Comedy Theatre. In addition, he is the executive director of Unscripted Learning.

Richie Ploesch, MA, BCBA, has been working in the field of special education for over 15 years. His specialty is educating students and young adults with autism spectrum disorder. Richie is the program director of Unscripted Learning.

IMPROVISED THEATRE AND THE AUTISM SPECTRUM

A Practical Guide to Teaching Social Connection and Communication Skills

GARY KRAMER AND RICHIE PLOESCH

Routledge
Taylor & Francis Group

NEW YORK AND LONDON

Cover image: © Getty Images

First published 2022
by Routledge
605 Third Avenue, New York, NY 10158

and by Routledge
2 Park Square, Milton Park, Abingdon, Oxon, OX14 4RN

Routledge is an imprint of the Taylor & Francis Group, an informa business

© 2022 Gary Kramer and Richie Ploesch

Library of Congress Cataloging-in-Publication Data
Names: Kramer, Gary, author. | Ploesch, Richie, author.
Title: Improvised theatre and the autism spectrum : a practical guide to
    teaching social connection and communication skills / Gary Kramer and
    Richie Ploesch.
Description: New York, NY : Routledge, 2022. | Includes bibliographical
    references and index.
Identifiers: LCCN 2021022503 (print) | LCCN 2021022504 (ebook) |
    ISBN 9781032075518 (hardback) | ISBN 9781032075501 (paperback) |
    ISBN 9781003207627 (ebook)
Subjects: LCSH: Children with autism spectrum disorders—Education. |
    Improvisation (Acting) | Games. | Social skills in children—Study and
    teaching. | Drama—Therapeutic use. | Drama in education.
Classification: LCC LC4717 .K73 2022 (print) | LCC LC4717 (ebook) |
    DDC 371.94—dc23
LC record available at https://lccn.loc.gov/2021022503
LC ebook record available at https://lccn.loc.gov/2021022504

ISBN: 978-1-032-07551-8 (hbk)
ISBN: 978-1-032-07550-1 (pbk)
ISBN: 978-1-003-20762-7 (ebk)

DOI: 10.4324/9781003207627

Typeset in Adobe Garamond Pro
by Apex CoVantage, LLC

CONTENTS

PREFACE

The sold-out audience started arriving early, and it was getting warm backstage. The lights were on and the speakers were playing a soft, easy melody to set the tone. We were in the crowded green room with 15 students reviewing some last-minute notes before the beginning of the show. No one was rehearsing lines that were pre-written because there was no script. They were preparing for a completely improvised, 90-minute performance.

These were not typical students, however. Every one of them was either on the autism spectrum or had a diagnosis of a related disorder and was a participant in a social skills program, which uses improvised theatre as its foundational tool.

Some of these students had language delays as children, others had crippling social anxiety, and yet, through the program, they had learned to communicate better, read social cues, and express themselves more clearly. And now they found themselves in a place that their families would not have foreseen . . . on stage in front of a live audience.

One by one, the students were greeted on stage with a sensory-friendly level of applause. By the time the performance was over, there was not a dry eye in the house. The audience, made up mostly of family and friends, rose to their feet, amazed at how deliberate the performance was, and how focused, communicative, and hilarious the students had been throughout. Their emotional response made it hard to maintain the sensory-friendly applause as the pride and joy felt at seeing their sons and daughters complete such a tremendously difficult and brave performance was overwhelming.

Imagine someone's son, daughter, or student attaining the same level of growth that would allow them to succeed in such a program. How might you help them achieve that accomplishment? Can this program be codified and replicated, in an easy-to-follow format, to reach more individuals worldwide? This book is the result of answering those questions.

In March 2017, Richie Ploesch and I were having drinks next door to the National Comedy Theatre following a rehearsal for our improvised comedy show, which had been running for almost 20 years in San Diego. We were discussing Richie's work as a BCBA (Board Certified Behavior Analyst), and what techniques he uses to work with individuals on the autism spectrum. What he described included the concepts of active listening, eye contact, recognizing verbal and physical cues, keeping conversation in the same realm, and acknowledging and accepting other viewpoints.

We both quickly realized that these concepts lined up exactly with the core concepts taught in improv theatre training. The question then arose, "What if there was a way to adapt improv training so it could be used formally in a setting for individuals on the spectrum?"

Within the year we had formed a non-profit organization, Unscripted Learning, and embarked on researching and developing a curriculum, and subsequently teaching classes to kids and teens with ASD. The program caught on quickly, and has continued to thrive and grow as more parents find out how well this approach works.

Improv allows students to leave behind the behavioral scripts that they are so often taught as young children, and instead react to real-world scenarios, which are always unscripted. The fun and play aspect of the training also helps mask the deeper lessons that are woven within.

This book is the result of hundreds of hours of preparation and classroom time spent experimenting with different exercises and activities designed to teach communication and social skills using the same techniques that are found in improvised theatre. Many of the activities result in genuinely funny moments for the students, and we have watched their confidence in communicating, not only with each other but in front of groups of people, grow tremendously. We hope that this book acts as a guide and reference tool towards creating a vibrant curriculum for educators seeking to teach social skills, creative thinking, and communication in a fun and engaging way.

Gary Kramer, Executive Director
Richie Ploesch, Program Director

ACKNOWLEDGMENTS

We would like to thank the following people and organizations for their help and guidance in creating our program, and for their continued support, both moral and financial.

Raquel Benguiat, Andreea Borcea, Cliff Boro, David Brown, Susan Clausen, Alex Deddeh, Sue Faber, Inna Fishman, PhD, Josh Hermsmeier, Steve Hohman, Mikaela Kinnear, PhD, Betsy Lenahan, Caitlyn McTaggart, Katherine Paszek, Beth Ploesch, Gary Poon, Dave Pressler, Anna Rowland, Laurel Schulz, and Jonah Weinberg.

Also, the fine folks at Autism Society of San Diego, Autism Speaks, Foundation for Developmental Disabilities, National Comedy Theatre, National Foundation for Autism Research, Nordson Foundation, Protostar Group, and Samuel I. & John Henry Fox Foundation.

And all of the parents and students of Unscripted Learning.

ABOUT THE AUTHORS

Gary Kramer is a producer, director, and actor, and is the artistic director and founder of the National Comedy Theatre, as well as executive director of Unscripted Learning. His production of the National Comedy Theatre is currently the longest running show in San Diego history, with over 6000 performances since opening in 1999. In addition to the San Diego production, Gary also directed the New York company of the show and has taught extensively for over 30 years. He has participated in countless shows across the country, as well as internationally. Gary has also served as executive director and vice president of the Board of the San Diego Performing Arts League.

Richie Ploesch, MA, BCBA, has been working in the field of special education for over 15 years. His specialty is educating students and young adults with autism spectrum disorder. He earned his teaching credential in 2006, a master's degree in 2008, and became a Board Certified Behavior Analyst in 2009. Since then, he has not only taught special education classes but also has taught as an adjunct professor, consulted with family members internationally, and provided in-home behavioral therapy to improve social skills and increase independence.

CHAPTER 1

INTRODUCTION

Many books written about improv are written solely about the games.

This book, however, is meant to dive deeper into the concepts that are taught using improv and how those concepts can help individuals with social skills deficits. This isn't merely a list of improv games and how to play them. This is a view into the world of teaching social skills to individuals with autism and other related special needs. We wanted to demonstrate the use of theatre-style improv and how the practices that make good improvisers can also make connected and social individuals. In other words, how we can use improv to teach us to build better social relationships.

In this book, we break up each game into multiple aspects, teach each one of those aspects, and then tie them all together so that anyone can play the game or use the skills in their daily lives. Improv is about inclusivity and is a way to teach students of various abilities. Many of these games were designed to fill a gap for our students and are not common to the improv world. By dissecting each game in an intentional way, we have a format that will help teach these traditional games to non-traditional learners.

The critical aspect of this program is not that we have a list of hundreds of games. It is that we have the intention of doing the little things right every single session. We handle the little things to create routine and consistency with every class meeting. This is a huge aspect to the program that makes it work. The structure we provide allows for the highest level of discovery during each game – this is

DOI: 10.4324/9781003207627-1

when learning happens. By following the routine, students can focus on the skills they need to improve upon, rather than exhausting their mental energy following a changing process. We often take for granted how flexible thinking can be very mentally taxing. There is a deliberate philosophy behind how we address that and other concerns for our students.

Philosophy

There are many common attributes in both improv training and autism education. In each of these, there is a focus on improving social awareness, recognizing verbal cues, and non-verbal communication. For the students in each of our classes, this comes down to a few main lessons. Active listening, understanding emotions, and flexibility in thinking are just a few of the things that students in both groups need to learn. The skills that make us good improvisers are the very skills that make us socially connected members of society and so should be taught to students with autism.

Throughout this book we are going to break down these topics and others. In order to share with you the thought process, it is first beneficial to understand the philosophy behind the program and the reasoning for each of the structural concepts.

Teens and young adults with autism often struggle from isolation and co-occurring diagnoses. These additional diagnoses can include mental health challenges that stem from the lack of social connectedness, including anxiety, depression, suicidal ideation, and other barriers. This is not from a lack of desire for social connectedness but a lack of opportunities and a lack of successes with these limited exposures. Various methodologies built into this curriculum have been systematically designed to address these challenges. Independent research has measured such attributes as anxiety, social competence, general wellbeing, and empathy. Positive growth has been demonstrated in each of these general areas of mental health in a relatively short amount of time. This growth is evident in both anecdotal data and qualitative data, but that does not mean we have all of the answers. We are sharing what has worked so far in the hopes that it will help and work for others.

The philosophy behind this curriculum comes from a combination of various sources. Our students have the potential to create endless connections and learning opportunities, and we've tried to do the same. So, we've pulled from multiple different sources to craft this environment. Play-based interventions combine with various mental health supports, and we pull proven philosophies from applied behavior analysis for a well-rounded, scientific approach. This curriculum will help disguise social skills therapy sessions as play and improv.

Play

For starters, it is well known that we all grow and develop by using play as a means for learning. Early learning and early discovery show that much of what we describe as play is really exploration of our immediate surroundings. This starts at a young age with cause-and-effect play, social play, and even word play. But our need for growth does not stop at an early age, but rather continues into our adulthood. Play is good for growing the mind and body, and this is an important key for us to understand in this program. We are teaching new skills, but doing so in game format leads to quicker acquisition of skills, long-term retention of these skills, and ease in generalizing these skills to novel situations. This is because play science tells us that as children with developing minds, play will fire neurons that lead to novel connections in the brain.

Many children with autism struggle with developing play skills at a young age. As a result, many early intervention programs invest heavily in teaching play and play imitation. However, as students enter early elementary age, the focus shifts to academic learning and structured social opportunities. There is less room for the mistake of saying too much, or speaking too loudly, or sharing off-topic information. This discovery is replaced with failure and isolation, which leads to withdrawal and limited success. Play is a way to reinvigorate enthusiasm for learning and attempting challenging skills. If you were to learn a new game, such as baseball, it would be more fun to go to a game, play a game, or watch a game than it would be to engage in drills for 3 hours a day. This is the approach we need to bring to our teens to reinvigorate the success and desire for learning. Play science tells us discovery is a wonderful teacher, and play leads to that exact discovery.

Mental Health

Mental health and wellbeing are not to be taken lightly. As mentioned earlier, our student population struggles with this, and that impacts each of our students and their families. By imbedding aspects of positive psychology, we are reframing the perspective of our students. Minor acts of gratitude have been shown to lead to major changes in someone's perspective of the world. By engaging in regular practice of sharing gratitude for small successes, we are shaping our mindset to focus on the good things that have happened instead of the negative things. It is hard to see how sharing about a delicious apple can make a difference, but that small readjustment leads to larger shifts and a more positive outlook overall. This is similar to a gratitude journal that so many people are now keeping – it helps train individuals to see the good in what is happening.

Each class starts with a daily moment of positive psychology in the form of sharing one small positive thing that has happened. We often think that good things have to be these large occasions (trips, new cars, straight A grades), but we forget that getting a good night's sleep is good as well.

Additionally, each class starts with a moment of mindfulness by sharing a brief meditation exercise. This consists of taking two deep breaths and helps ground us. This also acts as a separation between the world outside of our safe zone and the world within. In the outer world, we need to focus on being correct. In our class, confidence is the right answer and that leads to more success. By engaging in this brief act of meditation, we are allowing ourselves to acknowledge that the environment is changing, and we can change with it. We are also accepting that in this safe space we are not judged and thus can be our true selves, which is a freeing experience (for students, teachers, and parents).

Environment

To set up this engaging environment that is inviting, welcoming, and judgement-free, we pull from some teachings of applied behavior analysis (ABA), as well as general didactic teaching methodology. We discussed setting up visual and kinesthetic activities to remind us of change, but it is also effective to include for some very common ABA strategies. By writing a schedule and reviewing it prior to starting, you are allowing students to focus their working memory on the games rather than the structure of the class. When they feel self-doubt, they can find reassurance in knowing what is coming and when. Students do well with these expectations being outlined ahead of time and this eases tension. By shifting that off of their working memory and mental capacity, they can focus on the games at hand and allow themselves to learn and discover. The structure of the class allows for maximum discovery of the lessons presented in play.

The basic tenets of didactic teaching include a concept of scaffolding, which many of you may already understand. The concept of scaffolding is that you are building on previously mastered skills. In order to do this, you must first teach various skills. In this environment, if you haven't taught it, don't expect it. Students will fill in the gaps with their own creativity, but you must provide the structure, the insight, the knowledge, and the clarity of expectations. Without these things the students will get lost and your lessons won't make sense.

The final and possibly most important aspect of this entire curriculum is the concept of a debrief. For many of us we have an internal voice that we use to discuss how things went – from job interviews, to dates, to parties, to trips to the grocery store. We have an ability to debrief the successes and failures of each event. What went well? What stood out? Would you repeat those same choices? Was the experience worth your energy? If you cannot conduct this internal debrief, you cannot grow and learn from your experiences. Our students struggle with this debrief and we must model this discussion for them to help them learn this skill both during improv and during normal daily experiences. This then allows typical daily interactions to become learning opportunities.

Formula

One topic we have not yet discussed is our formula for funny. This is a concept that will come up regularly during your classes. This is not meant to be the driving focus of your class, but it is a good thing to highlight for students as they are finding success (or not) during each week. In order for a joke to be funny it must meet three criteria: be on topic, be specific, and be said with confidence.

If a joke is two of the three, it may be funny but is more likely to fall flat. For example, a strong statement that is specific and said with confidence but which is not on topic will shock the audience, confuse stage partners, and devolve the scene. This example happens frequently with students who are not sure what or how to contribute. They are often looking for a "right" answer or forcing a joke from another context. Reminding students of these three characteristics for a successful joke will help them be appropriate with their jokes and not force them into scenes.

The coming sections are written with these concepts in mind. Each game has these practices built into the structure and flow. At the end of this book, there is a sample, outlining approximately 6 weeks of classes. Keeping in mind all of these factors (scaffolding, preparing the environment, using the formula for funny) you will be able to use your existing skills to create a successful learning environment.

Within a few weeks of joining the group, we knew that my daughter had found the right place to be. She was the only girl in the group at the time. It was pretty obvious that, before she joined, the boys had gotten used to a certain kind of humor, which is perfectly understandable. One of the students made a joke that made her feel uncomfortable. She spoke up, advocating for herself, and explained that she wasn't okay with that kind of thing. What impressed us was that one of the older group members could see that she was still upset, so he stepped in and explained to the other boys why that joke was inappropriate. Once they were told how she felt, not only did the boys accept the explanation, they quickly apologized, and that kind of thing never happened again.

The members of the improv group build a bond as they work together to overcome their challenges while enjoying each other's sense of humor. After being part of the group for a couple of years, her birthday rolled around, and she decided that she wanted to invite the other kids to a birthday party. It was the first time in many years that she invited people to a party and was not confident that people would attend. It was the best birthday she ever had. Not only did all the kids show up, but the event prompted the creation of other outside activities, further building the friendships that started in improv.

Jane, Parent of 18-year-old teen

CHAPTER 2

STRUCTURE OF CLASS

Each class follows a set protocol that incorporates all the philosophies mentioned earlier in a modified and digestible way.

In this section we will outline the standard process for each class and the reasoning behind it. We will mention various therapies and provide scripts of things to say and highlight. The details for each game are included later in the individual descriptions of them. For now, this chapter is all about the overall structure of each class. Know that every aspect of this structure has a purpose, a "why" to speak of. This section explains each "why" so that the instructors have a deeper understanding and can replicate the structure and the therapeutic intent of that structure.

The summary for each class follows.

First 5 Minutes

The first 5 minutes or so of each class are reserved for casual conversations among staff and students. This is really an opportunity for staff to "check in" with students to see how they are doing. These conversations are a very enlightening and critical aspect of trauma-informed care, and are used by many schools in their multi-tiered systems of support. By conducting the informal check in, you are building rapport with students, they are building rapport with each

DOI: 10.4324/9781003207627-2

other, and you are learning student stressors – all under the disguise of a casual conversation. Greet each student. Encourage students to connect to each other and have playful, engaging conversations. Require students to put away devices and share with each other. Spend an extra minute or two checking in with students who have had a difficult time over the past week or at a previous class. Review the written schedule or rules if students need it. This 5 minutes is all about your relationship with each student. If you don't have a relationship with them, they won't trust you when you ask them to be vulnerable on stage.

Opening

There are several parts to the opening, but overall, the opening only takes about 5–10 minutes. Everyone stands in a circle on stage for the entirety of the opening.

The first thing you do is engage in a moment of mindfulness, starting by closing your eyes and taking two deep breaths. The script is the same every class: "Let's start by closing our eyes and taking two deep breaths . . . (inhale, exhale) one more . . . (inhale, exhale). Great! That's our cue to leave everything out there, out there, and just be here." That script has been repeated hundreds of times in exactly that fashion. It models mindfulness practices for the students, reminds other staff why we are there as a group, and acts as a grounding exercise before class starts.

The next exercise is a practice in positive psychology, whereby all participants share the smallest positive thing that happened since the last class. This feels strange at first, so be flexible as students are getting comfortable, but ultimately, we want the smallest positive thing (not the trip to Disneyland or the vacation we just went on). As mentioned earlier, this helps our students focus on the positive aspects of their day/week instead of hyper focusing on the negatives. It is very easy for our students to get "stuck" seeing the negatives. This is one way to shift that thinking.

Next, the schedule for the day is reviewed. The general plan for the day has already been written on a white board or some other visible format for all students to see. If students need an individual schedule, you can either provide that here or during the first 5 minutes of class in a private conversation. This helps alleviate anxiety for students about what is coming, when, and in what order, etc. This will then allow them to focus all of their attention on the games.

Warmup

The purpose of the warmup game is less about achieving a goal and more about a feeling. If students are relaxed, laughing, and engaged with each other, you have accomplished your goal. You are simply spending a few minutes to get the improv muscles warm and flexed. The goal is not to get things right, just to get them ready to think differently. These are short exercises (generally 5 minutes, but can go a minute or two longer/shorter depending on the mood of the group). Don't be afraid to end a warmup on a good laugh. That energy will carry into the rest of class.

As part of the warmup, we add in the concept of "failure" and what that really means. Students occasionally get so focused on doing an exercise perfectly that they are unable to pivot when things don't go as planned. It's not a failure if, during a game, someone makes a mistake. In fact, most of the warmups depend on mistakes being made frequently and then diving right in again.

To shake off any mistake, we use the "Aa-Ooh-Ga" technique to restart every game. The technique involves everyone putting their hand in the center of the circle (similar to a sports team before a game) and all saying the phrase "Aa-Ooh-Gah!!!," which is the sound of an old-time car horn. Everyone throws their hand in the air, and then we start again. It's a fun way to clean the slate and immediately start again without allowing anyone to dwell on an error.

Game/Debrief

This process is the cornerstone of the class and is meant to be repeated as many times as necessary. The general format of each game is that you introduce the game first, give a few examples, answer some questions, and share the concepts of the game. Then, allow students to participate as outlined in the individual game section. Afterwards, debrief each game. Discuss what worked, what didn't, what students learned, and why we play this game. There are more details available in the individual sections, including topics to highlight, but this is the general format to follow and an easy one to rely on if the group is stuck. Occasionally the debrief will get into an in-depth conversation. That is entirely OK and a welcomed part of each class. Do not end a debrief early to get to the next game. It is more important to dissect the conversation than it is to play the next game – you can always play it next week.

Closing

This process is similar to the opening in that it involves everyone being on stage in a circle. During the closing, everyone in the circle shares either a) one thing they liked today or b) one thing they learned. This is the "check out" process, where you get to see how students are ending the class feeling and if their mood has changed at all from the onset of class. This is also an opportunity to hear their insight into what stood out for them and what you could build upon in the future. Feel free to praise student efforts along the way as the group shares, but keep this section positive, particularly as it is a whole-group activity.

The lead teacher always shares last and generally provides a few words of insight about the day. Highlight something that stood out, whether it be an effort by the group, the attempts at a new character or game, the general tone of the class, etc. This is a chance to shape future classes by providing reassurance, praise, or constructive feedback of what could be better next time. Also, have the humility to share something that stood out to you. By modeling the vulnerability of sharing that, you are allowing them the same opportunity in the future.

The Unscripted Learning program has really been a godsend for my son. It's the only activity he's ever asked me to sign him up for, vs. me strongly suggesting it. Such a great opportunity and vital experience. When class was able to take place in person, I would see him on the stage working through the improv and being brilliant. It made my heart so happy! I also saw it making his heart happy as well! He would talk to me about each class on our drive home afterwards. He loved to relive the moments and laugh all over again. I can tell he is still getting a tremendous amount of experience and it's keeping his communication skills sharp. He still looks forward to class each week.

Everyone in his immediate life has noticed the change in his confidence since starting the class, and his ability to communicate with more ease. The program has definitely given him the platform he needed to help develop the communication skills he was lacking.

My husband and I couldn't be more grateful for the Unscripted Learning class. It has meant all the difference in my son's growth and confidence. It's truly given him the tools he needs in his toolbox as he transitions into adulthood and independence.

Barbara, Parent of 17-year-old teen

CHAPTER 3

THE GAMES
WARMUP GAMES

Every improv class begins with a quick series of warmup games that typically last 5–15 minutes in total. There are a number of reasons as to why these are utilized, and each activity addresses specific skills.

It begins with creating a safe space, where the issues outside of the rehearsal studio or classroom are left at the door. Starting with a blank slate and remaining "in the moment" is a basic tenet of improv, and running through a quick series of silly and fun exercises is a positive way to introduce any class.

There are a myriad number of warmup games available, and we have outlined several popular examples in this curriculum. The games are designed specifically to do the following:

- Create a common shared voice among the participants
- Allow the participants to "fail" at an unimportant task so that they get used to the concept of not being afraid of failure, and instead embrace the possibility
- Wipe clean the events of the day outside of the studio
- Jump start everyone's mind to allow them to begin to think quickly

There are several pitfalls that can happen in the warmup process that are very common. You might find that students can get hung up on rules or on being right or wrong in a warmup exercise. Students might become frustrated with themselves or count the number of times that they make a mistake. Occasionally you will see a game slow to a crawl as the students desperately attempt to be overly accurate.

DOI: 10.4324/9781003207627-3

The solution to any of these challenges is to explain to the students that the object of the games is to push ourselves to the limit of failure, and to be able to laugh at the failures of a silly game. If they are going slowly and accurately, they are not actually doing the game. The point is to move so quickly that an error is made, and then we attempt to do it again, but even faster. There is no "winning" in a warmup game – the only win is to go faster than the last time – and nobody is counting errors.

Surprisingly, this is a difficult concept for many students, and it can be addressed very early on in the rehearsal or teaching process. The games are designed so that most of them have a "failure" built in, and we all have an equal chance of "failing" at the games with no judgment.

BUNNY

STRUCTURE OF ACTIVITY

Students stand in a circle.

DURATION OF ACTIVITY

2 minutes

EXPLANATION OF ACTIVITY

One player starts by holding their hands on either side of their head (as if they are showing moose antlers) and quickly says "Bunny, Bunny, Bunny, Bunny" (they can repeat "bunny" as many times as they like for a few seconds). The person on their immediate right is doing the same thing but only holding up their right hand, and the person on the left is using their left hand, so there are three people participating, taking their lead from the central person. After a few seconds, the center person "passes" the bunny to someone else in the circle by clapping their hands together and pointing to the new person. That person takes up the bunny, along with the person on their right and left, and the game continues. The bunny is passed around the circle in this manner for a couple of minutes. Each person who receives the bunny moves a bit faster.

PURPOSE OF ACTIVITY

This game is all about laughing and being silly. Getting students to let their guard down is a great skill and will make class more enjoyable for them and for you. This is a great way to remind students to just have fun and be silly (and that it is OK to laugh).

TIPS FOR COACHING

There is no need to rush in this game, but if you can get the groups going faster that will make things a bit more fun. Also, some students might be a bit hesitant at first. That is OK, but work to get them more involved.

DEBRIEF

There is no need to dwell on this game too much. Maybe talk with students about how they felt before the game and after. Are they more relaxed now and, if so, do they recognize that being silly helped them get there?

GO

STRUCTURE OF ACTIVITY

Students stand in a circle with one person in the center of the circle.

DURATION OF ACTIVITY

1–2 minutes

EXPLANATION OF ACTIVITY

Students stand in a circle with one student in the center. The student in the center points across the circle at another student, says their name, and walks over to take their place within the circle. The selected student walks to the center of the circle and points to a new person, and the process continues.

PURPOSE OF ACTIVITY

This game is great at teaching students to remember each other's names while moving around the stage and the circle. This is also good for practicing making mistakes and doing so in a fun and light way. It is also a good mechanism for making clear choices and communicating clearly to others on stage.

TIPS FOR COACHING

Have the students move as quickly as possible and attempt to point to a new person each time they get to the center of the circle. It's easy to suddenly forget someone's name while under pressure, so make sure they can laugh it off if this happens.

DEBRIEF

Only do a debrief for the first several times you play this game. When doing a debrief, talk to students about how they felt when they were called into the middle of the circle. Explain that the feeling of being on the spot is ok and will go away over time as they get more comfortable, but in that moment, encourage them to make a bold choice and remember that if others laugh, that is OK. People will laugh at the things you do and say on stage, that is part of the reason for doing it. Remind students not to confuse that with people laughing at them as individuals.

Happy/Sad

STRUCTURE OF ACTIVITY

Students stand in a circle.

DURATION OF ACTIVITY

5 minutes

EXPLANATION OF ACTIVITY

Students stand in a circle. The first student can turn to their right and say "Happy!" or to their left and say "Sad!" This command then continues and is repeated in the same direction, keeping the same emotion, unless a student reverses direction by saying the other emotion. Additionally, as they pass the command, they say the word happy or sad while playing/feeling that emotion.

As a variation, a player can also say "Anger," and point across the circle as an alternative to Happy or Sad.

PURPOSE OF ACTIVITY

This is a quick and easy way to get students showing some emotions. Emotions are so important in improv and in life. The aim of this game is to get people saying and showing emotions in a playful way.

TIPS FOR COACHING

Encourage students to show their emotions in various ways. There are multiple levels of each of these – they can dial up or down the physicality, facial expressions, tone, volume, etc.

DEBRIEF

There is not a big need for a debrief after a warmup game like this, but it is always good to check in with the group about how they felt showing various emotions and what they noticed from others. Were other students more vocal? Less physical? More animated? etc. Use this information to guide you as you play more scene games later.

NAME GAME

STRUCTURE OF ACTIVITY

Students stand in a circle.

DURATION OF ACTIVITY

3 minutes

EXPLANATION OF ACTIVITY

Students stand in a circle. The first student will say their name and then say ". . . and I like _____." The blank represents something that they actually like to do. For example, it might be, "I'm Robert and I like to play tennis." The student will then quickly pantomime what it is they like. So, Robert might show a couple of seconds of hitting a tennis ball. The rest of the students would then say, "Hi Robert," and mimic hitting a tennis ball as well. The following student then takes a turn and it continues around the circle until everyone has introduced themselves.

PURPOSE OF ACTIVITY

This game is a way to help students learn each other's names. This is also a fun, silly introduction into the class and an easy way to welcome new students. This exposes students to pantomime, which will be very challenging for them later.

TIPS FOR COACHING

This game is good to play a handful of times when a new student joins the class or when a new class is starting. It does not need to be played more than a couple of times but can also be good after a short break. You can also add a theme if needed (for example, what you ate for lunch), which gives a slightly different take on this game.

DEBRIEF

Keep this debrief short. Ask students how they felt when pretending to do the activity. Spend a couple minutes talking about the pantomime piece and praise them for trying to demonstrate various actions. Then move on to more games.

RED BALL

STRUCTURE OF ACTIVITY

Students stand in a circle.

DURATION OF ACTIVITY

2–3 minutes

EXPLANATION OF ACTIVITY

The teacher will call out a student's name and then say "Red Ball" and mime tossing them a ball. That student calls out another student's name and repeats the gesture. Once the imaginary ball is moving along smoothly, the teacher starts a second ball in progress by calling out a student and saying "Green Ball." The object is to keep both imaginary balls in play at the same time. For very advanced students, a third ball can be entered into the game.

PURPOSE OF ACTIVITY

This game is an introduction to pantomime. It is designed to start learning pantomime without challenging students to do too many things all at once.

TIPS FOR COACHING

Allow for mistakes and some silliness to keep this light and fun. This part of improv is very hard. Also, go slowly to start with and only introduce one ball at a time.

DEBRIEF

Talk about how it felt to pretend to hold the different types of balls. Were they able to "feel" the weight of each one? Did they throw each of the balls differently? What were the differences between the two of them?

WHOOSH BONG

Students stand in a circle.

3–5 minutes

Students stand in a circle. One student begins by saying "Whoosh!" to their right or left. The student who the Whoosh was passed to can either continue passing the Whoosh in the same direction or they can say "Bong!," which would then reverse the direction so it goes back to the previous student.

Additional variations include saying "Highway!," in which case they can pass the turn across the circle to another student that they point at, or "Ramp!," which skips a player and proceeds in the same direction to the following player.

To get students listening to the whole group and paying attention to everything going on. Additionally, this game allows for students to make mistakes in a fun way while not having to worry about being right. This is also good for developing clear communication.

Start with just "Whoosh" and "Bong" as your only statements. Gradually introduce "Highway" and then "Ramp." Try to discourage the same students from saying the same command to the same people, so that they have to change it up to work on flexibility.

Not much debrief is needed after a game like this – it is more about getting students laughing and forgetting their normal daily routines and stresses for a moment.

ZIP ZAP ZOP

STRUCTURE OF ACTIVITY

Students stand in a circle.

DURATION OF ACTIVITY

5 minutes

EXPLANATION OF ACTIVITY

Students stand in a circle. One student begins and points at another random student and says "ZIP." That student then points to a new student and says "ZAP." In turn, that student points to a third and says "ZOP." The process then repeats as fast as the students can go. If they make an error, students all say "Aah-Ooh-Gah" (the sound of an old-time car horn) and whoever made the error starts again with ZIP.

PURPOSE OF ACTIVITY

Zip Zap Zop is a simple activity that is typically done first in a warmup. It is a chance for everyone to speak in a unified voice, to move quickly without overthinking, and to deal with failure of a very simple activity without repercussion.

TIPS FOR COACHING

Explain to students that the purpose of the game is to move as fast as possible rather than being concerned with being "correct." There is no way to win at this game – the only rule is to move quickly, shake off the failure, and then try to move quickly again. Students will naturally slow down to get it "right," so always push them to move faster. If the game is completely accurate, over and over, the students are not moving fast enough.

DEBRIEF

A debrief is only needed when first introducing this game. Once students have an understanding of the game, do not debrief as you will lose the momentum of the warmup. To get started, use the game to initiate conversations about eye contact, paying attention, communicating clearly, and making mistakes. Share that it is OK for mistakes to happen on stage and that we shouldn't let them impact our confidence or slow us down. Talk about how students feel doing the "Aah-Ooh-Gah" and discuss failing big on stage and HAVING FUN!

SCENE WORK/ STORYTELLING GAMES

The most complex, and typically most popular, improv games involve the idea of creating a scene or a sketch, seemingly out of thin air. This is done through the process of collaborative thinking, where each person is responsible for a small bit of the growing story and the participants all contribute.

In addition to the major concept of saying "Yes, and . . ." to an idea (see *Yes, and . . . Interview* game later in this section for further detail on this concept), creating a scene or story generally involves finding some kind of story arc. What is the beginning, middle, and end of the story, and how can we find that quickly when we don't know what the story will be about?

The generally accepted outline of any story is that we begin by learning who our characters are and what their situation is. The story then continues through a series of increasing challenges (in storytelling this is known as rising action), before hitting a climax and then wrapping up (known as the "denouement").

In improvised theatre, we can follow this general structure if the students can quickly establish who their characters are, what their relationship is to each other, where the story is set, what the ground rules are for the universe that the characters live in, and finally what it is that each character is after. This will help to create conflicts in scenes, which are all part of the rising action.

Stories typically have a narrative whereby we follow the exploits of one or two of the characters as they move through their respective journeys. By keeping in mind how stories are told, we can create a platform to tell a cohesive story that both the students and audience can follow.

It's a very good idea for students to find narratives that develop out of some level of truth, rather than just fantastical ideas that are not grounded in any sort of reality. Virtually every movie, play, or book can be broken down into a central theme, and the story arc can be discovered. For example, Star Wars is ultimately about a family squabble and individuals dealing with their acceptance or rejection of their destiny. It follows several characters, all of whom grow and face increasingly difficult challenges, which they may or may not successfully overcome.

When well-known stories such as this are broken down into their components, it's easier for students to see how stories are told and to incorporate those concepts into their scenes.

Conceptually, scene games and storytelling games can help tap into how individuals view the world while allowing them to use a character to speak in their voice and express their feelings and opinions.

3-LINE SCENE

OVERARCHING SKILL

Scene work; "Yes, and . . ."

STRUCTURE OF ACTIVITY

Two people are on stage at a time. The rest of the class can be in lines on either side of the stage or sitting in the audience.

DURATION OF ACTIVITY

5–10 minutes

EXPLANATION OF ACTIVITY

Player A makes a statement about their location. Player B presents a challenge based on their location. Player A then presents the solution to the challenge. The scene does not have to be exactly three lines, but it should be short.

EXAMPLE

A: I can't wait to dive into those waves!

B: Oh no! I forgot to bring sunscreen. We're going to get burned.

A: Don't worry, I brought an umbrella so we can be in the shade.

PURPOSE OF ACTIVITY

Starts to build the group-thinking mentality needed for longer/more advanced scenes, addresses "yes, and . . ." as a concept, helps with beginning scene work as it teaches students to not just say where they are but to interact with where they are, and also helps develop quick thinking.

INTRODUCTORY MODIFICATIONS

Start with familiar places. You may also need to provide the players with problems as well.

ADVANCED MODIFICATIONS

Use less familiar places, allow the scenes to go for more than three turns, or build in more pantomime.

PITFALLS

Many students start by saying specifically where they are instead of alluding to where they are (i.e., "Wow, the zoo is nice!" rather than "I can't wait to go see the zebras.")

TIPS FOR COACHING

This game is an important building block for scene work. Be encouraging of students and remind them that, on stage, any answer is the right answer. You can work on more nuanced skills later – the focus here should be on students building something together and creating a reality with their scene partner.

PREREQUISITE SKILLS

N/A

FUTURE SKILLS

Any scene game

DEBRIEF

This will be the first time some students have been on stage. Talk about how it felt to build a reality out of nothing and create something with a partner. Some students will try to overcomplicate this, so have them focus on simplifying it and allow for back and forth. This isn't about what one person can create; it is about what a team can create.

ABC

OVERARCHING SKILL

Scene work; justification

STRUCTURE OF ACTIVITY

Two students on stage create a scene. Each line has to start with the next letter in the alphabet.

DURATION OF ACTIVITY

15 minutes

EXPLANATION OF ACTIVITY

Four students will stand on each side of the stage. Two students take the stage and receive a suggestion from the class. One student says the first line, which begins with the letter "A." The other student responds with a line beginning with the letter "B," and so on. When they reach "Z," the letter is repeated and then they go backwards through the alphabet. If a player cannot come up with a line, or if they say a line that begins with the wrong letter, the teacher says "rotate" and two new students replace them in the scene.

EXAMPLE

Suggestion is video games. One student starts miming playing a game. Student 1: "Are you ever going to give me a chance to play, Susan?" Student 2: "Boy, you really are getting annoying, asking me all the time." Student 1: "Can't you see that I really want to play?" Student 2: "Don't keep bugging me, or I'm telling mom . . .," etc.

PURPOSE OF ACTIVITY

Scene work; justification; working on character development and relationships between characters; persevering through a game without giving up; thinking quickly.

INTRODUCTORY MODIFICATIONS

To get students started, you could just get them to deliver two to three lines each and expand from there.

ADVANCED MODIFICATIONS

Start from various places in the alphabet so students are not reliant on ABC as their initial lines. This will be particularly useful if students start to fall into the same lines over and over.

PITFALLS

Many students will get stuck on the alphabet aspect of this game. Also, students should be encouraged to go quickly but also add context to the scene, with meaningful lines/details. A series of short sentences/questions back and forth isn't fun to watch and doesn't add any depth to characters or scenes (i.e., "Are you sure?," "Because . . .," "Can you call mom?," "Depends"). Make sure they don't get caught up in the game and lose the scene aspect.

TIPS FOR COACHING

Students should not spend too much time trying to think of the "right" word. The faster they throw themselves into the scene, the more success they will see. Not being able to come up with a word to fit the correct letter is one of the fun parts of the game. Also, the more they establish what the scene is really about, rather than just two talking heads going through letters, the more interesting the scene will be. Lastly, encourage them to expand on their sentences during the scenes. Remember, they must start each sentence with the next letter of the alphabet, but they don't have to stop there. The sentences can be a bit longer, but they need to remember to give opportunities to their scene partner as well.

PREREQUISITE SKILLS

General scene work and character skills; some "yes, and . . ." skills

FUTURE SKILLS

N/A

DEBRIEF

When debriefing with students, check in with them about the challenges of this game. Talk about the scene as a whole and how it developed. Did the alphabet aspect of this game change how the scene unfolded? How did they find the balancing act of staying within the limitations of the game but still making the scene relatable and enjoyable?

AUDIENCE SOUND EFFECTS (SFX)

OVERARCHING SKILL

Flexibility; justification

STRUCTURE OF ACTIVITY

Two or three students create a scene while a fourth student offstage provides sound effects.

DURATION OF ACTIVITY

15–20 minutes (3–4 minutes per scene)

EXPLANATION OF ACTIVITY

Teacher picks a suggestion and two or three students create a scene based around that suggestion. During the scene, the players set up situations where a prop or the location might require a sound effect. At that time, an off-stage student will provide the appropriate sound. The students on stage have to justify why the sound was not necessarily accurate while continuing the scene.

EXAMPLE

Two students are doing a scene that takes place in Hawaii. One points offstage to a third student and says, "Isn't that one of those hula dancers?" At that point, a fourth student (the off-stage sound effects person) might provide hula music while the third student enters the stage and does a short dance. The third student welcomes the two students already on stage and says: "Thank you for coming to Maui. I know you really wanted to take a helicopter tour of the islands – here comes a helicopter now." The sound effects person would then do their best interpretation of a helicopter noise. Scene continues for 3–4 minutes.

PURPOSE OF ACTIVITY

This is a scene game that requires an extra level of flexibility. Generally in scenes, you work with your partner to create an alternate reality. In this set up, there is an additional layer of flexibility in that the sound effects can alter the course of the scene or the environment. This also means that students have to justify what is happening based on the sound effect.

INTRODUCTORY MODIFICATIONS

Make one or two sounds that are related and flow nicely with the scene. This will help students understand how the game works and be more successful at future attempts.

ADVANCED MODIFICATIONS

Make noises more regularly, and have noises come from abnormal objects or noises which suggest that something has gone amiss in the environment (e.g., go to start the car and it meows; the player then has to justify why there is a cat in their car).

PITFALLS

Some students will let the scene be completely controlled by the sound effect. This might derail their train of thought or motivation. Others will ignore the sound effect completely. Try to get students to find the right balance between working with the sounds and justifying them.

TIPS FOR COACHING

Remind students that, as a character, they have a motivation and should stick to that motivation. If they are motivated to get to work, every justification should come from that mindset. The sound effects should come out of what's going on in the scene, rather than random objects that can make sounds.

PREREQUISITE SKILLS

Basic scene work

FUTURE SKILLS

N/A

DEBRIEF

Discuss what worked and what didn't. Some students will like the sounds as it adds to the scene, while others will be derailed by them. Find the right balance for each student and work to get quality justifications.

BECAUSE

OVERARCHING SKILL

Group mind; justification

STRUCTURE OF ACTIVITY

Students sit in a circle and create a narrative story.

DURATION OF ACTIVITY

5–10 minutes

EXPLANATION OF ACTIVITY

Students sit in a circle. One person begins with a statement and then each subsequent student begins their statement with the word "because" and adds to the previous statement. Game continues in a circle until it reaches a logical conclusion.

EXAMPLE

Student 1: I went to the grocery store because I ran out of milk.

Student 2: Because I had cereal for all my meals today.

Student 3: Because I never learned proper nutrition in school.

Student 4: Because I was more interested in learning about robotics than nutrition.

Student 5: Because I want to build robots to take over the school.

Student 6: Because I got picked on in gym class and my robots will get my revenge, etc.

PURPOSE OF ACTIVITY

Justifying what was previously said and creating a shared world.

INTRODUCTORY MODIFICATIONS

Start with just two exchanges.

ADVANCED MODIFICATIONS

N/A

PITFALLS

Students often make the next sentence unrelated to the previous so the story does not make sense. They should focus on the previous sentence and build a justification based on that.

TIPS FOR COACHING

This is one, giant, run-on sentence that tells a story in reverse order. It builds a new reality with just justifications. Try to have students focus on justifying only the previous sentence without worrying about what came before.

PREREQUISITE SKILLS

Story

FUTURE SKILLS

Other justification games; more complex storytelling

DEBRIEF

This game can unravel quickly and become very silly and disconnected. When debriefing, work to get students to stay on topic and relate their sentence to the one right before it. This is an exercise in listening and justification that will tell a story from end to beginning. It can get very nonsensical, so work to have student justifications tie to the reality of the previous line.

BLIND LINE

OVERARCHING SKILL

Creating on-topic answers based on the context of a scene, relationships, and a situation

STRUCTURE OF ACTIVITY

Two or three students on stage create a scene using occasional dialogue provided by the audience.

DURATION OF ACTIVITY

15–20 minutes

EXPLANATION OF ACTIVITY

Two or three students leave the room so they cannot hear the subsequent discussion. Teacher gets six to eight lines of dialogue (song lyric, famous quote, punchline to a joke, ad slogan, etc.) from audience members. Each line is written on a separate slip of paper, then folded and randomly set on the stage. When the participating students re-enter the room they create an original scene, inventing all the dialogue, based on a single new suggestion from the class. However, at certain points during the scene, a student can pick up a line from the stage floor and read it out loud as their line of dialogue. That student then needs to justify why they said that out-of-context line and continue the scene as seamlessly as possible.

EXAMPLE

During a scene that involves a disagreement between siblings, one student might indicate that they have an important point to make. The other student picks up a line that might say "I'll be back." He or she might then immediately leave the stage. The student can re-enter the scene at a later point, indicating why they had left previously (i.e., "I had to ask Dad's point of view on this").

PURPOSE OF ACTIVITY

Practicing justifications that are on topic and relevant; thinking quickly and creatively; understanding one person's decision-making process and bringing back all relevant information to that view point; perspective taking; theory of mind.

INTRODUCTORY MODIFICATIONS

Make the sentences very vague to ease pressure of justification; only give students one line to justify in a scene; use sentences that may be familiar to the student.

ADVANCED MODIFICATIONS

Get specific lines from various media (i.e., movie lines, quotes, book lines, Bible verses, song lyrics, etc.).

PITFALLS

Students might need help with initiating the scene and could become reliant on you for prompts. Try to fade that support out as quickly as possible to teach them the rhythm of the game. Students also have a difficult time with lines that do not fit nicely within the scene or context. Don't let them get hung up on being perfect – their job is to do the best they can with the current situation. The "line" often pushes students away from their thought process. They might need some coaching (i.e., guided questioning) to help them come to a justification.

TIPS FOR COACHING

All the lines should have some sort of narrative quality to them. Make sure students don't set up a pre-justification for the lines – the lines should stand alone (i.e., don't say "My dad always said [line] . . ."). When students are giving a justification, coach them to stay relevant to the topic if they begin to stray from it.

PREREQUISITE SKILLS

Justification skills; scene work skills; some understanding of characters is a plus

FUTURE SKILLS

More advanced justification games (e.g., *Pan Left/Pan Right, Blind Freeze*)

DEBRIEF

When debriefing after this game, make sure you talk about what worked with the justifications. Continue to guide students to give an on-topic justification. You may need to give other examples of what could have been said so students hear other ideas and expand their thinking. This game is really challenging, so don't push feedback too much, but continue to help them discover what works for them.

BOARD GAME

OVERARCHING SKILL

Creating a common reality with others

STRUCTURE OF ACTIVITY

Students are broken into small groups of three or four.

DURATION OF ACTIVITY

20–30 minutes

EXPLANATION OF ACTIVITY

Students get into small groups and are given 10–15 minutes to create a new board game. They need to come up with a title, how the game is played, the object of the game, pieces or props that are needed to play, and how to win the game. They then explain their game to the class and answer questions.

EXAMPLE

Students come up with a game called Turtle Crossing. They decide that the object of the game is to get your turtle from point A to point B, avoiding crocodiles that can be placed by other players. The game is played with dice and a board that shows a river, turtle, food, hazards, etc.

PURPOSE OF ACTIVITY

By having to work together and use each other's suggestions, groups are forced to listen to each other and expand on ideas. This creates a collaborative environment for people to practice contributing and building on previously discussed aspects of the game. This is a good game for "yes and," but while working collaboratively with others.

INTRODUCTORY MODIFICATIONS

Use a game that the students already know and create a modification of that game (i.e., Monopoly, but with food items instead of street names).

ADVANCED MODIFICATIONS

Allow students to create an app-based game, which opens up more conversations and opportunities.

PITFALLS

Students will force in their own ideas without listening to others and creating something together. This means that one person is not only doing all the work, but they are dominating the creative aspect. Work to have players volley ideas back and forth while including each other's suggestions.

TIPS FOR COACHING

Have students embrace all ideas so they can act as springboards for the creation of other ideas for the game. This game is very much in the "yes, and" tradition – there are no bad ideas and each should prompt an additional idea rather than conflict. Start with the name of the game and work from there.

PREREQUISITE SKILLS

N/A

FUTURE SKILLS

Advanced "Yes and" games; other collaborative-type games

DEBRIEF

Discuss why we play a game like this with students – games like this are fun, but the lesson isn't always apparent to students. When playing this game we are working together to create an agreed-upon game and using our group mind to create something truly special and unique, which will never be created again in the future. It is also an exercise in sharing the idea-creation process and in justifying each other's ideas.

COMMERCIAL

OVERARCHING SKILL

Confidence on stage while making up ideas on the spot

STRUCTURE OF ACTIVITY

One student at a time on stage creating a sales pitch for a simple object.

DURATION OF ACTIVITY

1–2 minutes per student

EXPLANATION OF ACTIVITY

Students take to the stage one at a time. The teacher then suggests a very simple object and the student must do a 1-minute sales pitch for that object, describing, in great detail, all of the features. Students can describe either very realistic or out-of-the-box, creative ideas in their pitch.

EXAMPLE

The object suggested is a pencil. The student explains that it is made from sustainable wood, hand painted and sharpened, and each pencil has the signature of the pencil maker on it. It has impressive erasable qualities and has built-in auto correct, etc.

PURPOSE OF ACTIVITY

Being comfortable giving details about a topic is a critical skill for any improviser. By forcing someone to talk for an entire minute, they have to give greater detail, expanding their explanations beyond the norm, and create some new realities.

INTRODUCTORY MODIFICATIONS

N/A

ADVANCED MODIFICATIONS

Allow for Q&A afterwards. Also, adding in a special characteristic or history to the item is a way of adding a more challenging twist.

PITFALLS

Students tend to pick things they are comfortable with, which is OK for the first round. Once they are comfortable, however, try to push them to describe different and more difficult items so they don't get stuck trying to "be right." Also, students tend to trail off at about the 30-second mark, so give them a heads up when they are halfway to encourage some new thinking.

TIPS FOR COACHING

Encourage students to free-associate and to specifically think about what would make the object more appealing. Are there other uses for the object, outside of the obvious? What additional features might the object have that set it apart from what we expect?

PREREQUISITE SKILLS

N/A

FUTURE SKILLS

N/A

DEBRIEF

Revisit a few of the moments that stood out as particularly interesting and discuss why they stood out (if there was something funny about a game, what made it funny?). If people struggled, discuss why they struggled and what made it easier for some students and harder for others. Also, for some students it will be easier when they have an item or topic that they know nothing about. Discuss as a group how, when students are on stage, they are the expert and anything they say is the correct answer as long as it is based in the reality created on stage.

DISASTER

OVERARCHING SKILL

Creating a scene in a newly constructed reality

STRUCTURE OF ACTIVITY

Two students on stage creating a scene, with twists added by the teacher.

DURATION OF ACTIVITY

5 minutes per pair

EXPLANATION OF ACTIVITY

Two students on stage are given a specific location. They create a scene in their location and, once the scene is established, the teacher will suggest a disaster related to their location. The students have to continue the scene, dealing with the new information and applying it to the structure of their relationship.

EXAMPLE

Students are given the suggestion of a sailboat. They begin a scene where they are on a long voyage at sea, and one has taken the role of captain. The teacher then suggests the disaster of the mast falling over and disappearing into the ocean with all the sails. The students then have a conflict as to who should be in charge, since there's no longer a sailboat captain if there's no sail. They explore the idea of loyalty vs. mutiny while trying to keep the ship from tipping over.

PURPOSE OF ACTIVITY

By changing the flow of the scene, students are forced to adapt and adjust their reality. They have to problem solve based on their character and make decisions based on the limitations of their situation. It forces flexible thinking and adaptations based on what stage partners, other performers, or the audience suggest.

INTRODUCTORY MODIFICATIONS

Give students the location and disaster information ahead of time and allow them to talk about their options for responding to the disaster before they are on stage, letting students work together to pick what they might do. This alleviates some of the stress of them coming up with solutions on the spot but still forces them to work together.

ADVANCED MODIFICATIONS

N/A

PITFALLS

Students will try to just leave the stage when presented with the disaster. Or they will come up with solutions that are not necessarily an option in that environment (i.e., fly away from the fire but not put it out).

TIPS FOR COACHING

Work to have students create realistic answers that are based in the reality that was created. Students will start to use super powers (or cartoon solutions), which eliminates the challenge of keeping the scene based in reality.

PREREQUISITE SKILLS

Basic scene work; pantomime skills

FUTURE SKILLS

More advanced scene games that involve manipulating the environment

DEBRIEF

Talk to students about what worked and what didn't with regard to their solutions. Encourage students to stay in the disaster and not have a "fly away" type answer. Remind them that every answer doesn't have to be a well thought out plan – there is still fun in exploring failed solutions.

DR. KNOW-IT-ALL

OVERARCHING SKILL

Collaborative thinking; listening; appropriate dialogue

STRUCTURE OF ACTIVITY

Three students on stage responding to questions from the audience.

DURATION OF ACTIVITY

10 minutes

EXPLANATION OF ACTIVITY

Three students stand on stage shoulder to shoulder, facing the audience – these students make up the "doctor." The teacher gets random questions from the audience about any general subject, and the students on stage answer one word at a time, with each student only saying one word before it is the next student's turn. They continue in this way until they reach the end of the answer. This process is repeated for three or four questions.

EXAMPLE

Question from the audience might be, "Why is the sky blue?" The "doctor" might answer: "The-sky-is-blue-because-it-makes-it-easier-to-see-clouds."

PURPOSE OF ACTIVITY

To develop listening skills, "Yes, and . . ." skills, and group thinking to give detailed, on-topic answers to various questions.

INTRODUCTORY MODIFICATIONS

Make sure questions involve general topics and do not have simple yes or no answers. Questions can be from all disciplines, from science to sports to philosophy.

ADVANCED MODIFICATIONS

A fun "bit" to add is to have the team bow in unison at the end of each answer. It's an ironic and funny moment.

PITFALLS

To start, many students don't actually answer the question or are afraid to commit to an answer. Remind them that they are the expert and any answer they give is the right answer. Encourage them to give that answer with confidence and pretend they really do know it all. Students will shy away from that at first but will become better in time.

TIPS FOR COACHING

Tell students to answer as quickly as possible without searching for the "right" word. Students should face the person who asked the question when providing the answer.

PREREQUISITE SKILLS

N/A

FUTURE SKILLS

Helps to build on "yes and . . ." as a skill; builds on group thinking; is helpful for future games like *Expert* where you know all the answers versus being given questions about a given topic.

DEBRIEF

Ask students why each round worked and discuss how actually attempting to answer the question, rather than trying to be funny, worked. Did answering quickly make the results more surprising and funnier? Also, this game builds on the skill of quickly combining the thoughts of all the participants – did the students actively listen to each other when answering?

ENTRANCE

OVERARCHING SKILL

Creating a quality scene

STRUCTURE OF ACTIVITY

One student on stage, second student then enters the scene.

DURATION OF ACTIVITY

5–10 minutes per pair

EXPLANATION OF ACTIVITY

One student begins on stage by creating their setting. The second student then enters after a few seconds, announcing some event that has just happened to them. The scene then continues with the two students reacting to what happened.

EXAMPLE

Student 1 is in a kitchen, student 2 enters and says, "Well, I just got fired." They then have to deal with the repercussions of that statement – why it happened, what the reasons were, how it relates to their relationship, etc.

PURPOSE OF ACTIVITY

The purpose of this activity is to get students to make strong choices for their characters and use those choices as motivation for the scene.

INTRODUCTORY MODIFICATIONS

Help students come up with big events that may have happened prior to the game to help drive their character.

ADVANCED MODIFICATIONS

Student 2 enters the stage but does not tell of the event that has just happened. Instead, they can give clues with what they say or how they interact with their stage partners or the environment.

PITFALLS

Students tend to get fixated on what just happened rather than use that as a guide for their character's current emotional state. If something amazing happened, then yes, your character will be hyper focused on that. However, most of the time, the events could be minor but will drive the character without taking over every aspect of who they are.

TIPS FOR COACHING

Make sure the students choose big events that have some grounding in reality so that they can have strong reactions to them. They should react realistically to the information and see how it affects their relationship with their on-stage partner. The student who enters the scene doesn't necessarily have to "announce" what happened, but it should be clear that they are dealing with an event that will eventually come out in the conversation.

PREREQUISITE SKILLS

Basic scene work

FUTURE SKILLS

N/A

DEBRIEF

When discussing how things went, make sure to check in regarding what worked about the student's on-stage decisions and what didn't. Also feel free to discuss what decisions they made and how they were able to bring those decisions into scenes. This game is an exercise in character development, so feel free to encourage them to explore new types of characters and push the boundaries of their comfort zones.

FAMILY TRADITION

OVERARCHING SKILL

Using information as a scene generator

STRUCTURE OF ACTIVITY

One student on stage describing an event. Two other students then act out the story.

DURATION OF ACTIVITY

5–10 minutes per group

EXPLANATION OF ACTIVITY

One at a time, students take the stage and describe to the group a family tradition that they have, real or imaginary. After they describe the tradition, two other students then create a scene in which they act out that tradition.

EXAMPLE

A student might describe a tradition in which when someone in their family turns 18, they are blindfolded and taken out to the woods, and left for a week with no supplies, having to fend for themselves, with only a knife, two pairs of socks, and a deck of playing cards. After describing this scenario, two students create a scene, with one student playing the dad and the other his son in their car. The dad says, "Son, Happy Birthday . . . I remember when your grandfather and I took this same drive, how much I looked up to him . . . now good luck," and pushes him out of the car. Other students might play a bear, a hermit, woodland sound effects, etc.

PURPOSE OF ACTIVITY

To practice hearing information that is being shared and using it to create scenes. The scenes should be based on the information, although it doesn't have to be an exact translation.

INTRODUCTORY MODIFICATIONS

After you get a story from one student, discuss as a group all the different people and characters that could be involved. Then get two people to pick characters from that list and use that to get their scene started.

ADVANCED MODIFICATIONS

To build on information in a different way, set a rule that students cannot act out the scene exactly as it was just described. So, if the description was Thanksgiving Dinner, you could show characters involved getting ready for dinner, after dinner, or sharing with their friends what happened at dinner, but you cannot show the actual dinner itself.

PITFALLS

When students make up a tradition it tends to be extreme and nonsensical. Maybe start by having them share a real tradition to help base these in real life. Also, students tend to show exactly what they heard and forget about conflict, characters, motivation, emotions, and environment. Encourage them to keep all these elements within a scene.

TIPS FOR COACHING

Students should listen closely to the story to be able to capture all of the details in the scene. A great idea is to pick up on the theme of the tradition (e.g., is it dangerous, silly, adventurous) and then let the scene reflect that theme.

PREREQUISITE SKILLS

Basic scene work

FUTURE SKILLS

Long-form games

DEBRIEF

When discussing this game, make sure to highlight how the scenes were related to the tradition. Also, it is important that the person sharing the tradition give lots of detail and specifics so that the players can incorporate those into the scenes. This helps with idea generation and brings more life and flavor to the scenes.

FRESH CHOICE

OVERARCHING SKILL

Justifying the changes that come within a scene

STRUCTURE OF ACTIVITY

Two to three people creating a scene on stage.

DURATION OF ACTIVITY

5 minutes per game

EXPLANATION OF ACTIVITY

Two or three students are given a suggestion and begin a scene. Periodically, after a student has said a line, the teacher can call out "Fresh Choice," and the student that just delivered the line will immediately say a different line than the one they previously just said. The teacher can call "Fresh Choice" several times on a line, so the student might have to deliver the line three times with different content each time. The other students then need to react to the fact that the last line spoken might not have been what they expected and attempt to continue the scene.

EXAMPLE

Two students create a scene in which they're setting a table in a dining room.

Student 3 then enters the scene: "Mom, Dad – I just made Dean's List!"

Teacher: "Fresh Choice."

Student 3 re-enters: "Mom, Dad – I got kicked out of college."

Teacher: "Fresh Choice."

Student 3 (re-entering, walking as if they have big shoes on): "Mom, Dad – I've decided to join the circus and pursue my dream of being a clown."

The scene then continues with the parents dealing with that decision.

PURPOSE OF ACTIVITY

The purpose of this activity is to teach students to adapt and take the scene in a new direction. Often players forget to be flexible in their decision making and conversation, but in this game, they have to show adaptability based on whatever has become the new reality.

INTRODUCTORY MODIFICATIONS

Start with easy changes and allow for minor adjustments.

ADVANCED MODIFICATIONS

Give players specific things to change about their line (e.g., "fresh entrance" "fresh reaction").

PITFALLS

Students will likely change only slight details instead of making larger changes (e.g., "I have two cats" . . . "Fresh Choice" . . . "I have three cats") to begin with. Students also get stuck on coming up with ideas to change for the "Fresh Choice." Encourage them to go with something similar, then opposite, then different, then just anything if they are getting stuck (e.g., cat, dog, polar bear, sasquatch).

TIPS FOR COACHING

Tell students that they can change either the CONTENT of their lines (the specifics of what they're saying) or the INTENT of the line (why are they saying it). Frequently, a simple change of mood will help the student come up with a new line. The students should all react to the final line said.

PREREQUISITE SKILLS

Basic scene work; justification

FUTURE SKILLS

N/A

DEBRIEF

During debriefs, discuss which scenes became nonsensical and which ones stayed on topic. Sometimes the fresh choice can be such a drastic switch that we lose the grounding of the scene. Which scenes held their original motivation and which ones became lost in the fresh choices. As players become better at this game, they will be able to make new choices but keep the reality of the scene present.

HAPPY BIRTHDAY

OVERARCHING SKILL

Combining "Yes, and" with pantomime to create a quality scene

STRUCTURE OF ACTIVITY

Two players on stage in a very short scene.

DURATION OF ACTIVITY

3–5 minutes per group

EXPLANATION OF ACTIVITY

One person gives an awful birthday present to the other. The student receiving the gift loves it and adds on to it, escalating the level of awfulness. They then continue back and forth in a short (even as short as four sentence) scene, utilizing the idea of the gift as an idea generator for the scene.

EXAMPLE

Student 1: Happy Birthday! I got you a huge bag of nails.

Student 2: Excellent! I was about to make a bed of nails for my yoga instructor, and I was all out!

Student 1: I heard he has a roommate, so I got you enough nails to make bunk beds of nails.

Student 2: We can use the nails to hammer it together as well. I see there's a number on the back to order more. We can use my phone of nails to call customer support.

PURPOSE OF ACTIVITY

We are working to show the audience how we interact with an item and how we can have a conversation that is not entirely focused on the item. We can discuss the history of the item, why it is important, the specifics of the item, how much the person giving the gift cares about the receiver based on the item, etc.

INTRODUCTORY MODIFICATIONS

You could start with items that people genuinely really would like to receive and expand from there.

ADVANCED MODIFICATIONS

Create a longer scene to see what happens in the interactions or cut to other times and places to learn more about each character.

PITFALLS

Students often give scripted answers (e.g., thanks, I've always wanted this). Push for details to be given and have them visualize what it is they are receiving. That will help them add to the conversation with details.

TIPS FOR COACHING

Students should listen to what their scene partner says and work off of that in a "yes, and" manner, rather than attempting to come up with random statements. Each line escalates what the previous line set up. They should also deal with the gift as a real object and pantomime holding it, using it, etc.

PREREQUISITE SKILLS

Basic pantomime; showing emotions; basic scene work

FUTURE SKILLS

Long-form style of games

DEBRIEF

Students often want to think and talk about what it was they received, but the real scene is about the interaction between two people and why one person is really motivated by this gift. The gift can be anything, as long as the student provides details, but the interaction between the characters is what keeps the audience engaged and laughing about the ridiculous gift.

LAST NIGHT

OVERARCHING SKILL

Developing "Yes and" skills to create a new story/universe

STRUCTURE OF ACTIVITY

Two or three students have a discussion and then present what they discussed to the class.

DURATION OF ACTIVITY

5–10 minutes per team

EXPLANATION OF ACTIVITY

Students get into groups of two or three and come up with a premise of something that happened the night before. They discuss and expand on details about that event as they all add information. After about 3–4 minutes, each group stands in front of the class and explains what happened the previous night, answering questions about specific details.

EXAMPLE

A group might come up with the premise that they stole the answers to an exam from the school garbage. One student says that they snuck into the school garbage room. Another adds that they were the one that distracted the custodian. The third adds that it was the answer key to tomorrow's algebra test. The first student is feeling a bit guilty and thinks they should tell their parents. The second says that they would get in trouble because she is the principal's daughter, . . . etc.

PURPOSE OF ACTIVITY

This game is all about staying in the reality that has been created and using "Yes and" to expand on that. By working together to create the story of what happened the night before, groups can experience varying points of view and emotional reactions to a shared experience.

INTRODUCTORY MODIFICATIONS

Start everyone with the same incident (e.g., everyone explains what happened after they went to dinner).

ADVANCED MODIFICATIONS

N/A

PITFALLS

Students often either stick only to what is true in their world or they jump to the extreme example of science fiction. Work to have them improvising in between these extremes, with some embellishment and creativity but grounded in reality. Also, one student generally uses up all the time and doesn't allow for others to contribute to the reality, so encourage students to contribute evenly.

TIPS FOR COACHING

Keep somewhat "normal" ideas to start with so that they can add information that they have some knowledge about. Each person only has to contribute one small thing at a time, rather than writing the entire story by themselves. Ensure that they acknowledge each other's information and incorporate it as they build the story.

PREREQUISITE SKILLS

Basic "yes and" games would be beneficial

FUTURE SKILLS

Story; basic and advanced scene work

DEBRIEF

When debriefing, discuss how students came up with their idea and how it can be used in a scene or other games. Discuss how groups can show that on stage in a scene and how the audience would enjoy seeing this story unfold. This is a great way to get people to develop "yes and" skills, so discuss how it works when in groups of two or three.

MORNING AFTER

OVERARCHING SKILL

Expressing your point of view by portraying emotions

STRUCTURE OF ACTIVITY

Three or four students come up with an idea out of earshot of the rest of the class, then they create a scene.

DURATION OF ACTIVITY

About 5 minutes per group

EXPLANATION OF ACTIVITY

A group of three or four students huddle together and decide on an event that happened the night before over the course of about 30 seconds. They then act out a scene in which they see each other the next day for the first time since the event. Each person will try to play a different point of view or reaction to the event that they were all part of. Afterward, the class tries to guess what it was that happened the previous night.

EXAMPLE

The students decide that the night before they snuck into the zoo and released a bunch of animals. One student might walk in morosely, feeling very guilty about it, a second might enter very excited about liberating animals, a third might want to post on social media about it, and the fourth might be paranoid that they are going to get caught. The four different points of view easily clash, which sets up a conflict within the scene.

PURPOSE OF ACTIVITY

To build a world using a group mindset and adjust your character's point of view based on the other characters around you. This also practices establishing a history with your stage partners, which makes something more worth watching for the audience. Furthermore, it expands on your ability to show emotions, ask questions, and build relationships with those around you.

INTRODUCTORY MODIFICATIONS

Teachers assign the event that happened.

ADVANCED MODIFICATIONS

N/A

PITFALLS

Often students say exactly what happened or what they saw; this is also true for when they make comments about where they are. Have students practice giving subtle clues and leading up to a reveal. This will build suspense for the audience and help the other characters develop who they are and how they feel about what happened. People like to see the different emotions and viewpoints interacting.

TIPS FOR COACHING

The students should not discuss their points of view ahead of time – they should spend just 30 seconds coming up with the premise, then improvise from there. If a student sees another with a point of view similar to what they were planning, they should quickly pivot to a different viewpoint. Also, there's no reason for exposition in the scene, so they shouldn't feel the need to point out to the "audience" what happened previously. The actors know, and that's all that is important. This activity is all about different reactions to events creating different points of view, which lead to dramatic conflict.

PREREQUISITE SKILLS

Basic scene work; emotion-based games

FUTURE SKILLS

Advanced scene work; other clue-giving games

DEBRIEF

When checking in with students, talk about how they created their events and the clues they gave. Not all clues are meant to give away the answer, but they can help the audience get closer to it. Our students struggle to find the balance between being too vague and too specific. Discuss what worked and what didn't, both from a character/emotional perspective and from a scene/clue-giving perspective.

PAN LEFT/PAN RIGHT

OVERARCHING SKILL

Listening to other scenes; line justification

STRUCTURE OF ACTIVITY

Three or four students create a scene while standing in a triangular or square formation (two students in front facing the audience and one or two at the back facing the back wall).

DURATION OF ACTIVITY

10 minutes

EXPLANATION OF ACTIVITY

Students form a triangle or square on the stage, with the students closest to the audience facing front and the students at the back facing the back wall. The front two students get a suggestion of a location, and the teacher will then tell the students to "pan left" or "pan right." The students then move one spot over to the side, similar to a revolving door. That will result in a new pair (one from the last group, and one new student) facing forward. They get a different suggestion and so on, until all three or four pairs have been given a different location. The scene then starts in one location and, at any point, the teacher can tell the students to pan left or right. When they do, the next scene begins, but the last line of dialogue from the previous scene gets repeated as the first line of the new scene – just in a different context and with different meaning. The game continues until each scene is presented two or three times, always with imaginary time having elapsed while the scene was not being viewed by the audience.

EXAMPLE

The three locations given: zoo, principal's office, and grocery store. Players A and B are at the zoo, B and C are in the principal's office, and C and A are in the grocery store. Scene begins:

Player A: "You know, my dad is the zookeeper here."

Player B: "That's really cool – is he doing anything about those monkeys running free?"

Player A: "Oh no, I better call him!"

Player B: "It looks like they're trying to escape."

Teacher: "Pan Left."

Player C: (taking on the part of the principal) "They're trying to escape!"

Player B: "Tell the students that they better not leave or they will get detention."

Player C: "Good idea, Mrs. Ploesch. Remind me to promote you to vice principal," etc.

PURPOSE OF ACTIVITY

In addition to general scene work, a big part of this game is the justification of the new line. Not only do the actors have to remember what their scene was about, but they also have to incorporate whatever was in that line and make it part of the scene. Being able to justify is a skill that is needed in a variety of games.

INTRODUCTORY MODIFICATIONS

It might be best to start with three students to help keep this short to start with. Also, it is good to repeat the line after you say "pan left" or "pan right." E.g., "Pan left, It is time for bed." This helps students who didn't hear the line or forgot it in the moment. It is also helpful to use suggestions for places that students are familiar with at first.

ADVANCED MODIFICATIONS

Work up to involving four people and get more varied suggestions. Instead of suggesting four places in the city you live in, for example, use one place you've always wanted to visit, one place from fiction, one place in your home town, and one business you'd like to own. That adds in a layer of complexity for the audience and for the students.

PITFALLS

Many students will not be able to justify the line based on their character's perspective. Make sure to coach them on giving some type of justification based on their character's motivations and viewpoints. It will be hard to not have all the scenes start to have similar themes – try to encourage students to make four clearly distinct scenes with little overlap.

TIPS FOR COACHING

The gimmick of the game is the justification, which will be easiest when you have a good scene to build from. Focus on the characters and relationships within the scene and work to improve the justifications later.

PREREQUISITE SKILLS

Line justification; basic scene work

FUTURE SKILLS

If students are able to justify lines, they can plan games such as *Blind Line*.

DEBRIEF

When you debrief, talk about the justification, but also talk about the scene work aspect. This game only works when you have both elements, but it can be hard for students to juggle both aspects (particularly for new students). The audience likes to see people struggle with the justification, but not at the expense of a quality, realistically played scene. Discuss having different characters so that the scenes don't all bleed into one scene with people rotating in and out.

SHARK TANK

OVERARCHING SKILL

Creating a new reality and sharing details of that reality

STRUCTURE OF ACTIVITY

One student on stage presenting to the class.

DURATION OF ACTIVITY

About 2–3 minutes per student

EXPLANATION OF ACTIVITY

Students come up with an idea for a product and then pitch it to the class in a short monologue. They have to explain all the great features about the product and how it can change a person's life. The class then asks questions about the product, which the student answers.

EXAMPLE

A student might come up with the idea for Electric Pants. They then explain that they work by providing both heat and A/C when necessary, have a zipper that zips itself, and can assist with walking if the person is tired. The class might then ask how they are going to be marketed, what powers them, whether they are dangerous, etc.

PURPOSE OF ACTIVITY

This game helps students become more comfortable with public speaking and helps them build confidence in their ability to be on stage. By starting with a monologue, players are creating a new reality and speaking to each person in the audience. The Q&A that follows helps them develop their quick-thinking skills and stay within the reality of their newly created universe.

INTRODUCTORY MODIFICATIONS

Students could do a shorter monologue or the teacher could stand on stage with them and add in details as a level of support.

ADVANCED MODIFICATIONS

Have students work in pairs and present for a longer period of time.

PITFALLS

Students will want to bring in a conversation about money, but that isn't necessary for this game. Instead, have them focus on the creative aspect of sharing and using their energy in presenting.

TIPS FOR COACHING

Students should stand by their inventions and not worry about all the logical imperfections of them. The goal is to be confident speaking in front of the group and presenting an idea.

PREREQUISITE SKILLS

Some comfort in being on stage alone

FUTURE SKILLS

Advanced creating/explaining games (e.g., *Slo-Mo*)

DEBRIEF

Discuss with students what felt good about doing this exercise. Was it easier to give the monologue or answer the questions? Students will have different responses, which will encourage an open discussion amongst them. Also, some students will want to give a longer monologue. Ask them how they came up with their ideas so they can share with the group and everyone can learn their own process for creating new ideas.

SILENT TENSION

OVERARCHING SKILL

Pantomime; scene work

STRUCTURE OF ACTIVITY

Two students on stage creating a short scene.

DURATION OF ACTIVITY

Approximately 2–3 minutes per pair

EXPLANATION OF ACTIVITY

Students are given a suggestion of a location. They then create a short scene set at that location, but they are not allowed to speak for the first 30 seconds of the scene. They must create the opening of the scene without any dialogue, and then continue the scene for another minute or two.

EXAMPLE

The suggested location might be a gym. The two students act out working out near each other, but one seems to be frustrated with the other, although neither of them is saying anything yet. He continues to get more frustrated, shaking his head, sighing, etc., until after the 30 seconds, when he says, "I'm never going to be in the same shape that you are!" The other student replies, "Well, you need to actually lift heavy weights instead of that donut you've been lifting," and the scene continues from there.

PURPOSE OF ACTIVITY

Students will have to use skills other than verbal communication to establish the basics of a scene (their relationship, their viewpoint, their emotion). This forces them to pay attention to other cues and communication tools to get the scene started. This also allows them to create their environment and establish the location.

INTRODUCTORY MODIFICATIONS

Keep the silent time short and work to expand it. Also, teachers may need to give students some details before they start (emotion, location, job, etc.).

ADVANCED MODIFICATIONS

Challenge students to act out a full minute of the scene in silence.

PITFALLS

Students struggle to keep silent and start a scene at the same time – they can often do one or the other, but find it harder to do both together. As the teacher, you may need to coach them to get things started.

TIPS FOR COACHING

Students should not avoid the awkwardness of the silence, but rather use it to help drive the scene forward. Let them know that the silence is the most interesting part of the scene, where they can establish their relationship and location in a realistic way.

PREREQUISITE SKILLS

Scene work; pantomime; expressing emotions

FUTURE SKILLS

Other advanced scene games (e.g., *Pan Left/Pan Right*)

DEBRIEF

This game is challenging for several reasons, including the increased need for pantomime and the silent portrayal of emotions and decision making. Students will struggle with this game, and that is OK. Talk to students about what worked and what didn't. Have students elaborate on their ideas and discuss how they changed them once the scene started.

STORY

OVERARCHING SKILL

Using "Yes and"

STRUCTURE OF ACTIVITY

Students stand in a line across the stage, facing the audience.

DURATION OF ACTIVITY

About 10 minutes

EXPLANATION OF ACTIVITY

Students stand across the stage in a line, shoulder to shoulder, typically six to eight students at a time. The teacher gets the title of a new story and then points at the students one at a time. Students tell the story when they are pointed to and cut off when the teacher stops pointing. When a new student is pointed at, the story continues exactly where it left off, even if it is in the middle of a sentence or word.

Variations: this game can also be played one sentence at a time, or even one word at a time.

EXAMPLE

N/A

PURPOSE OF ACTIVITY

Students will have to work on creating a unique universe by combining listening skills, collective mind, and "yes and" skills. This means that if they have an idea, they may be able to work it in, but they may also be forced to abandon the idea. Students will have to learn to work together and share ownership of the story.

INTRODUCTORY MODIFICATIONS

Start by doing one sentence or one word at a time until students understand the game. This will help students with the structure.

ADVANCED MODIFICATIONS

Have students build on the story to include a moral, or have multiple chapters.

PITFALLS

Students often are not listening to their peers in a way that they can then expand on. Make sure students are paying attention and that when they add to the story, it stays within the agreed upon reality. The story will travel – make sure students aren't forcing an agenda as things develop.

TIPS FOR COACHING

Ask the students to visualize the story as it is being told, so that they are all on the same page. If you see a student push an agenda that is not in context with the story, encourage them to stick to the story that the rest of the group is telling. This game is all about collaboration and saying yes to everyone's ideas.

PREREQUISITE SKILLS

N/A

FUTURE SKILLS

Other advanced "Yes, and . . ." games (e.g., *Dr. Know-It-All*)

DEBRIEF

It is always a good idea to discuss each story and how the plot developed. You are not only discussing the story, but how the story developed or took a turn based on each player's contribution. Some students will bring in a forced agenda – discuss why that did or did not work. It is also a good idea to let students share what they had in mind so others can hear of different alternatives that were possible in that story.

THANKSGIVING TRADITION

OVERARCHING SKILL

"Yes, and" with creative thinking

STRUCTURE OF ACTIVITY

One student at a time on stage.

DURATION OF ACTIVITY

2–3 minutes per student

EXPLANATION OF ACTIVITY

Students step on stage one at a time and tell the class a Thanksgiving tradition their family has, real or made up. After they explain the tradition, the students can then ask two or three questions about the tradition.

EXAMPLE

A student might say, "Every Thanksgiving my family has a turkey leg throwing competition, where we go outside after dinner and we see who can throw the leg the farthest and with the most accuracy. It was started by my grandfather, who was a famous shot putter in the 1956 Olympic games in Melbourne."

PURPOSE OF ACTIVITY

To build confidence by presenting in front of an audience. Also to improve "yes, and" skills by answering questions and creating a new reality.

INTRODUCTORY MODIFICATIONS

N/A

ADVANCED MODIFICATIONS

N/A

PITFALLS

Students will either share a real example or make up an entirely random set of events that don't make sense – encourage them to describe a somewhat realistic tradition and give a clear explanation of events.

TIPS FOR COACHING

Students should choose a tradition that can be explained easily and succinctly. The more confident they are in their story, the more believable it will be. The game is all about speaking with confidence.

PREREQUISITE SKILLS

N/A

FUTURE SKILLS

Scene work; other creation games (e.g., *Story*, *Good/Bad Advice*)

DEBRIEF

Discuss with students how it felt to be on stage and answer questions. Did they feel comfortable projecting their voice or did they find this difficult. If they described a fictitious tradition, ask them if it was hard to come up with a new tradition and if it was based on anything from reality. Review what stage presence looks like (on stage, feet move quietly, speak confidently, project voice).

TRAVEL GUIDE

OVERARCHING SKILL

Creative thinking; audience presentation

STRUCTURE OF ACTIVITY

One or two students on stage facing the audience.

DURATION OF ACTIVITY

Approximately 1–2 minutes per student/pair

EXPLANATION OF ACTIVITY

A student, or pair of students, stands in front of the class and is given a made-up name for a country. They then proceed to describe to the audience all the reasons why someone would want to travel there, as if they were a guide book. They mention specifics about the country, including pros and cons of the country, traditional foods, customs, etc. The audience can then pose questions to the students after they have initially described their country.

EXAMPLE

Students are given the name of Pradastan. They might say that the country is famous for its fashion, so shopping is great, but it is expensive. It's best to go in the fall, since the colors of the trees match the bright colors of their garments. The food isn't very good, but there are a lot of nighttime activities and beautiful people there. Also, religion is very important to the citizens of Pradastan, with yearly pageants that celebrate victory over the devil, etc.

PURPOSE OF ACTIVITY

This game is designed to help students feel comfortable standing on stage, presenting to an audience, projecting their voice, and answering questions. This game also helps students with staying within the reality they have created and making up new details about that reality.

INTRODUCTORY MODIFICATIONS

For those who are struggling, they can make up just one aspect of the culture or the place instead of trying to create an entire travel guide.

ADVANCED MODIFICATIONS

For advanced students, or classes that want to expand, they can use this as a scene generator. As the presenter talks about a tradition or food, we can see a scene of other students bringing that to life. They would work together and play off each other to expand the reality.

PITFALLS

Students like to talk about places they have been and will often stick to the norm. Push them to expand their ideas and challenge themselves to come up with new foods, traditions, holidays, etc.

TIPS FOR COACHING

It's important for students to "yes . . . and" all their ideas, so that they flow naturally when they are talking, rather than trying to filter out only their best ideas. Each idea that they discover can fit into the bigger puzzle piece – if they allow each idea to inform the next.

PREREQUISITE SKILLS

N/A

FUTURE SKILLS

Scene games; other monologue type games (e.g., *Slo-Mo*)

DEBRIEF

For a game like this, some students can start with a place they have been and expand on that. Ask them how they came up with the ideas and how they brought them to life in their descriptions. Also, discuss what details brought those ideas to life. Get feedback from the audience as well. Discuss how it felt to be on stage and how they think they can improve on the content and their presentation.

UNIQUE ITEM

OVERARCHING SKILL

Presentation to an audience; creative thinking

STRUCTURE OF ACTIVITY

One student on stage talking to the class.

DURATION OF ACTIVITY

About 2–3 minutes per student

EXPLANATION OF ACTIVITY

A student will step on stage and describe a simple object that has unique qualities to it. They describe the object, what makes it different, its uses, drawbacks, etc. After describing it for a minute or so, the class asks questions about it.

EXAMPLE

A student might say that they have a wallet that always contains just enough money to pay for whatever they are buying. If they are buying food in a restaurant, it has exact change, plus tip. If they go to the movies, it has enough for a ticket, plus a small popcorn and drink. The drawback is that it is a little judgmental, and will not allow you to purchase items that you don't need. For example, if you are at a supermarket, it won't let you buy too much junk food but will have enough money for healthy foods only. It's like a financial life coach.

PURPOSE OF ACTIVITY

Presenting to a group is a challenge, but when you are discussing the magical qualities of an everyday item, it is a little more exciting and motivating. As a teacher, have students think about their stage presence, their demeanor on stage, the volume of their voice, how they are moving, etc. This is all part of being a good improviser but also part of having quality conversations in everyday life.

INTRODUCTORY MODIFICATIONS

Give students the item and have them explain the magical quality of it. Ask them some guiding questions like, "how did you get this item" or "how long has it been magical," etc.

ADVANCED MODIFICATIONS

Have students work in pairs and discuss how the item has been used for good and for evil. Also have them share the history of the item. This will make their presentation longer.

PITFALLS

Students have a hard time assigning creative powers to an item, getting stuck on the everyday use of the item. You may need to guide them and help them come up with creative ideas.

TIPS FOR COACHING

Students should just start talking about the item and logically follow where the description goes. There's no need to pre-plan or have a huge idea in advance – one aspect of the item will lead to another. All they need is the initial premise, and they can let the narrative flow from there.

PREREQUISITE SKILLS

N/A

FUTURE SKILLS

This game can be used as a scene generator for other scenes

DEBRIEF

Share with students things you noticed about their presentation and delivery. Remind them that being confident on stage is a big win, regardless of what they are saying when on stage. The formula for funny is a statement made on-topic, with confidence, and with details. Discuss how they could be doing that in these monologues and how you could use these ideas for generating scenes later.

VIDEO GAME

OVERARCHING SKILL

Creating a new universe

STRUCTURE OF ACTIVITY

Students in pairs off stage, then presenting on stage.

DURATION OF ACTIVITY

30–40 minutes for the class

EXPLANATION OF ACTIVITY

Students are paired up and have about 5 minutes to create a new video game. They then, in their pairs, step on stage and describe the game to the class. Afterwards, they create a short scene inspired by the game.

EXAMPLE

A team might come up with a game called Dentist. The object of the game is to clean as many teeth and fill as many cavities as possible while avoiding hazards. The hazards might be plaque monsters, being bitten by the patient, evil gingivitis, etc. They have weapons at their disposal, such as fluoride bombs and power floss. Each time they clean one set of teeth, a new set appears with more hazards. There's also an evil orthodontist that can show up and create more problems for the players (i.e., rubber bands, stuck food, etc.).

PURPOSE OF ACTIVITY

Working to create a new world with a partner requires listening and "Yes, and." Students have to navigate which ideas to push forward and which ones to let go of in that moment. This is great for working in teams and collaborating (skills that are important in life as well as improv). By practicing this game, students will become better at group projects, team work, and communication, including outside of improv.

INTRODUCTORY MODIFICATIONS

N/A

ADVANCED MODIFICATIONS

An advanced version of this game is to give everyone the same title. Then allow them to each create a new game based on that. Compare and contrast the different elements of students' ideas.

PITFALLS

Students get caught up in minor details and spend too much time thinking about things that won't move the conversation forward. Work with them to expand their thinking to generalities to get started. Also, students often like to work with ideas of games they already like (or ideas they've already had), but try to get them to come up with new games or concepts.

TIPS FOR COACHING

Students should simply start with a basic name for the game and then collaborate on how to escalate the challenges within the game. Each idea can be built upon, rather than thinking about why an idea wouldn't work.

PREREQUISITE SKILLS

N/A

FUTURE SKILLS

Advanced scene games

DEBRIEF

When discussing different games, make sure to talk about the plot and the setting of each game. Ask students how they came up with those ideas from the suggestion and have them share a bit about their discussion. Remember, you are using this to get them to work better as a team, discuss the concept of group mind, and recognize that these games are not one person's creation. These are concepts that will help with scenes later and will help with teamwork as well.

WORST CASE SCENARIO

OVERARCHING SKILL

Scene work; group thinking

STRUCTURE OF ACTIVITY

Two students on stage.

DURATION OF ACTIVITY

About 3 minutes per pair

EXPLANATION OF ACTIVITY

Two students step on stage and the teacher supplies them with a suggestion of a location. The first student establishes where they are, based on the suggestion. The second student then mentions a disaster, related to the location they are in. They then create a scene about facing that disaster.

EXAMPLE

Suggestion might be a boat. First student might say, "Honey, I'm glad we finally took that cruise that we've been talking about for years. It's going to be a great second honeymoon." Second student might say, "Sweetheart, any reason why the ship seems to be leaning to one side? Do you think it has anything to do with that hole in the hull?" They then create a scene where they have to notify the captain of the ship, figure out where the lifeboats are, grab their expensive luggage, turn off the Celine Dion background music, etc.

PURPOSE OF ACTIVITY

Practicing working together in a scene is very important for scene development. In this game, students work together to solve a problem with whatever tools they have available. This also allows the audience to see into their imagination and creativity.

INTRODUCTORY MODIFICATIONS

Give the scene and the disaster – the students then just work together to create the scene around these details.

ADVANCED MODIFICATIONS

N/A

PITFALLS

Students will often look for the most extreme solution (e.g., if there is fire, I must have a helicopter with 500 gallons of water). Instead, have them push for the most realistic solution that is readily available. That will help them develop teamwork in the scene and demonstrate their camaraderie to the audience.

TIPS FOR COACHING

Sometimes the easiest responses create the best scenes, rather than trying to overcomplicate or write the whole story in one sentence. The conflict of the scene isn't necessarily the disaster but what comes out of the disaster between the characters.

PREREQUISITE SKILLS

Basic scene work

FUTURE SKILLS

Advanced scenes and games (e.g., *Pan Left/Pan Right*)

DEBRIEF

Afterwards, check in with students to see how they felt their scenes developed. Did they get to the end too quickly? Did the scene build in suspense? Was there teamwork but also tension? Talk about the scenes and highlight the ones that had good depth and character viewpoints. Discuss whether the students liked their characters and if they felt their solution was based on the tools they had available.

YES, AND . . . INTERVIEW

Collaborative thinking; brainstorming; storytelling; saying "yes" to outside ideas

Teacher and student, or two students, sitting on stools/chairs on stage.

About 1–2 minutes per student

A student is brought to the stage and is endowed with being an expert at a non-typical subject that is suggested by the class. The teacher interviews the student about the subject by making statements to the student about their expertise. The first two words that the student speaks for each question are "Yes . . . And," and then they add a tiny bit of information to what the original statement was. The teacher uses their answer to formulate another statement and the process repeats for 1–2 minutes.

The suggestion is "shoelaces."

Teacher: "My guest here is Alex, and she is an expert on shoelaces. Now, Alex, I understand that you discovered that shoelaces around the world can tell us a lot about their various cultures."

Student: "Yes, and I realized that very often a shoelace from a specific country frequently is a symbol for their favorite foods."

Teacher: "You had said that the shoelaces of Italy, for example, closely resemble pasta in color and texture."

Student: "Yes, and in fact, red shoelaces are very popular in Italy, as it represents the sauce that goes over the pasta."

Teacher: "In fact, you've developed a partnership with the Ragu company to actually brand the sauce-colored shoelaces."

Student: "Yes, and the only issue is that children have been trying to eat the shoelaces, and the executives at Ragu are concerned about lawsuits," etc.

PURPOSE OF ACTIVITY

This activity is all about expanding on the conversation in a way that is still relatively on topic. In the shoelace example, all those statements are possible given that that person is an expert. Those occurrences are all a possibility for that person but are also all on topic to the conversation. It is important to be able to have flexibility in a conversation, but also be a contributor so the other person isn't doing all the talking (or listening). This game is about finding that balance and having a back-and-forth conversation.

INTRODUCTORY MODIFICATIONS

N/A

ADVANCED MODIFICATIONS

N/A

PITFALLS

Students can try to do too much work when adding on to the initial statements. They should only add one simple thing and then let the story progress naturally.

TIPS FOR COACHING

The "questions" to a student should always be in the form of a statement, rather than a question. The less that a student pushes, the more room for collaboration there is. Students should always work off the one piece of information that they most recently received from one another, rather than bringing in new information.

PREREQUISITE SKILLS

N/A

FUTURE SKILLS

Other interview style games; *Story*

DEBRIEF

Afterwards, ask students what felt good and what was a struggle. How did they feel being on stage and coming up with things to add to the previous statement? Did they feel it was hard to expand on the conversation? Was it hard to come up with details? Some students will enjoy this game and others will struggle with it. Talk about how students can use this in scenes and games going forward and explain that they don't actually have to say the "Yes, and . . ." part when using it in those contexts. This is a pivotal skill of improv and will be highlighted in many of the games outlined in this book.

PANTOMIME GAMES

One of the challenges in creating an improvised scene is that there are no props or set pieces available, perhaps with the exception of a chair or a stool.

This challenge, however, creates opportunities for a performer to create their own setting and props merely by suggesting them into the scene and dealing with them in a realistic way.

Most people associate pantomime with the traditional concept of a French mime in a striped shirt and made-up face, overly dramatizing their surroundings or doing set pieces, such as the stereotypical glass box.

In improv, however, we use mime to add props or to create our surroundings so that there is a context in which each scene can be created. If the scene is being played in a nebulous location, it is difficult or impossible to portray an honest reaction to whatever situation is being created.

We move, speak, and act differently based on our surroundings. For example, we would speak to our friends differently in a library than we would on the playground or in the principal's office. By using pantomime to help create our setting (in improv terminology, this is called "creating your *where*" or "creating your environment") we can create the framework in which a scene can be established.

The use of pantomime is best taught by instructing the students to actually imagine what it is like to hold and use a particular object, rather than using a stereotypical approach. For example, a phone may be held in a variety of ways depending on the type of phone. Most phones today are smartphones, so they are held differently than they would have been 20 years ago. The one way they are <u>not</u> held is by the traditional "thumb and pinky to the side of the head" indication that most people will show when demonstrating a phone. This creates an unrealistic use of the prop that neither the actor or audience believes, and doesn't allow for the performer to truly buy into their role. A phone being used with a weak signal is held differently from a phone being used to text or surf the web. Each different use of the phone says a great deal about the character, location, and situation.

Another common prop (and one which is used way too often in improv) is a gun. Most people will do the traditional "pointed index finger, thumb in the air" gesture to indicate this prop. However, how an individual holds a gun, and indeed what kind of gun it is, says a lot about the character being played, the situation, and the environment. A handgun held at the hip might indicate a film noir gangster, while a gun being held sideways might be a more contemporary character. A rifle looks different from a handgun, which is different from a bazooka. It's an easy jump to demonstrate how important it is to be very specific with pantomimed props and to actually use them as intended, rather than just providing an indication of the item for the benefit of the audience.

A popular exercise in pantomime is to bring in a few different props from home (i.e., coffee mug, phone, knife/fork/plate) and have the students pick them up one at a time and really study the shape of their hands as they hold each object, the challenge of performing a scene while holding them, and how that affects movement and tone.

Another exercise is in the use of doors. Having a pantomime door in a scene is a great way to ensure that entrances and exits are clean and specific, and that the action of a scene is taking place in front of the audience. Have students walk in and out of doors in the classroom, as well as the building if there are various types of doors (i.e., door knob vs. crash bar), and ask them to observe what their movement pattern is like in each instance. Students will be amazed at the swing of doors, how far a door moves, what it takes to open and close them, and, ultimately, how that might be incorporated into a scene.

By adding setting, walls, doors, windows, and props to a scene students will have a more realistic environment in which to create. It's probably the most overlooked concept to a new improv student, yet establishing a context to enable improvisation of a scene to begin is one of the most critical concepts. It is extremely helpful to know where a scene is taking place and what the limitations or opportunities are within that setting.

Lastly, it is important that all the actors remember that items placed in a scene take up physical space and cannot float or be porous. If a character is holding a coffee cup, it needs to be put down on a tangible object rather than just vanishing into thin air. Every person on the stage (and audience) will notice a character walking through a door that had previously been closed. Creating an awareness of solid objects on stage will help the performers to visualize and relate to the environment, and provide context for the scene to be played in a realistic way.

BUILD A __

OVERARCHING SKILL

Pantomime; group thinking

STRUCTURE OF ACTIVITY

Students sit in a circle, taking turns to add an element to the imaginary object that is being built. Alternatively, students could be sitting in the audience and each person steps on stage, one at a time, to add a new element to the object.

DURATION OF ACTIVITY

10 minutes

EXPLANATION OF ACTIVITY

Teacher decides on an object to be "built." One at a time, students come up with parts to be added to the object, and mime adding them, while telling the class what it is they are adding. At the end, the group discusses what worked and what parts might have been missing.

EXAMPLE

If the object was a car, the first student might add the steering wheel, second could add doors, third adds gas/brake pedals, fourth adds wheels, fifth adds engine, etc. Each part is described in as much detail as possible (e.g., it's a leather wheel, red doors, etc.).

PURPOSE OF ACTIVITY

There are two purposes to this activity. First, it promotes group thinking across the individuals, which will help later with more advanced scene work and activities. Second, introducing pantomime in a fun way will help students bring it into future scenes and practice a very challenging skill.

INTRODUCTORY MODIFICATIONS

Start by listing all the items that might be added. For example, if you are building a dog house you would need a floor, four walls, a roof, a dog bed, a water bowl, etc. Then, on their turn, students can pick one of these elements and pantomime adding it to the object.

ADVANCED MODIFICATIONS

Do not give an end goal in mind, instead see what the group creates. Try to make sure they are connected somehow, but allow the item to take on any shape or creation. You could also add in special attributes to the item (e.g., this is a box with a mirror on it and green jello inside, and it can use this antennae to see the future).

PITFALLS

It is challenging for students to stay on topic and build off what others have started creating. Also, students tend to force in their own ideas instead of working together and staying in the reality of what is being built.

TIPS FOR COACHING

Make sure students stay on topic and don't let their additions become too silly or unrelated to the object. Encourage students to visualize the finished object if they are having trouble coming up with an idea as to what to add.

PREREQUISITE SKILLS

N/A

FUTURE SKILLS

More advanced pantomime skills; other group-thinking games

DEBRIEF

It is OK if things get a little far-fetched the first round. However, as students discover how to play, try to reign them in and coach them to stay within the realm of possibilities. This is less likely to happen for the special attribute version, but can be a rule for the realistic version. Also, see if students can show the size and weight of an object in their pantomime (holding a tire is different than holding a tennis ball).

CHORES

OVERARCHING SKILL

Pantomime; confidence on stage

STRUCTURE OF ACTIVITY

Students individually on stage pantomiming simple chores.

DURATION OF ACTIVITY

Approx. 2 minutes per individual

EXPLANATION OF ACTIVITY

Students take the stage one at a time. The teacher suggests a specific chore and the student then carefully pantomimes all the steps involved in completing the chore while narrating what they are doing.

EXAMPLE

The teacher might suggest doing the laundry. A student would then pantomime separating the colors while describing what they are doing. Then they would carry the laundry to the machine, open the door, put the laundry in, etc. The entire time, they are narrating each step.

PURPOSE OF ACTIVITY

This game is about combining pantomime with narration and really forces students to show what they are doing while they are doing it. It is a good way to start working on pantomime, which is a challenging skill for many of our students.

INTRODUCTORY MODIFICATIONS

Pick shorter tasks with easy beginning, middle, and end points.

ADVANCED MODIFICATIONS

Pick longer tasks that require more complex movements and may be harder to demonstrate. You could also turn this into a group game where one person does the actions while the other narrates.

PITFALLS

Students have a hard time showing clear movements, which makes it hard for the audience to know what they are doing.

TIPS FOR COACHING

Make sure the students slow down and don't leave out any steps. Point out when they jump forward in time and miss important parts of each chore. Encourage students to imagine the weight and feel of each object that they are touching.

PREREQUISITE SKILLS

N/A

FUTURE SKILLS

Slo-Mo; using pantomime in scenes; gibberish games

DEBRIEF

When debriefing, highlight that when students slowed down and showed very clearly what they were doing, it was easier to view as an audience member. The purpose of narration is to help the person on stage pantomime with focus and clarity. Being able to use pantomime without narration is such a pivotal skill in improv, and games like this will be revisited multiple times.

GUESS WHAT

OVERARCHING SKILL

Pantomime

STRUCTURE OF ACTIVITY

One student on stage pantomiming to the rest of the class.

DURATION OF ACTIVITY

1–2 minutes per student

EXPLANATION OF ACTIVITY

Students come up with an object to pantomime to the rest of the class. One at a time, they step on stage and mime using that object. The class then guesses what the object might be.

EXAMPLE

A student pantomimes staring into a mirror and being concerned with what they are seeing. They then pantomime opening a drawer and removing an object. They hold the object in their hand and slowly run it through their hair repeatedly. The teacher then asks the class what the object is, and the class correctly guesses, "a hairbrush."

PURPOSE OF ACTIVITY

To practice slowing down and highlighting how we interact with objects when they aren't there.

INTRODUCTORY MODIFICATIONS

It helps if the teacher does an example and talks through what they are pantomiming so the students can see it. You could do a whole practice round of this if it helps the students feel more comfortable.

ADVANCED MODIFICATIONS

The presenting can be done in partners, but they would have to work together and follow each other's lead.

PITFALLS

Students struggle with pantomime in general. They often go too fast and don't show crisp, clean movements, which just confuses the audience. Encourage students to slow down and emphasize various movements to bring life to their gestures

TIPS FOR COACHING

Students should move slowly and deliberately. There is always a reason for using an object, so the students should begin by showing why they are holding that particular object (e.g., a button falls off their shirt, so they need to thread a needle and sew it; or they just woke up, so they need to brush their teeth).

PREREQUISITE SKILLS

N/A

FUTURE SKILLS

More advanced pantomime games and scenes (e.g., *Slo-Mo*)

DEBRIEF

This game can be challenging as the thinking involved is very abstract. Try to have students highlight what went well in this and encourage them to slow down and think about each step. Discuss as a group what it was like to be on stage and what it was like to be an audience member. Having had both experiences will help them when they pantomime on stage.

INVISIBLE SPORTS

OVERARCHING SKILL

Pantomime; gestures

STRUCTURE OF ACTIVITY

Students are paired up throughout the room.

DURATION OF ACTIVITY

5 minutes

EXPLANATION OF ACTIVITY

Students are put in pairs and scattered throughout the room. Each pair picks a sport and then pantomimes playing that sport with each other. After a couple of minutes, the teacher can ask them to then pick a different sport and repeat the exercise.

EXAMPLE

If a pair picks hockey, one might be pantomiming skating with the puck while the other is guarding a pantomime goal.

PURPOSE OF ACTIVITY

Working on pantomiming skills will help students bring scenes to life. This is a way to practice using those skills. This also enhances abstract thinking and imaginative skills, which can both be very challenging for students.

INTRODUCTORY MODIFICATIONS

Start slow and pick a game with few moving pieces. It is also nice to have the teacher narrate a round while all the students pantomime together. This will help them slow down and exaggerate movements.

ADVANCED MODIFICATIONS

Have students work together in small groups and try to create a realistic game play.

PITFALLS

Students often rush through pantomiming and it creates sloppy scene work. This also makes it hard for others on stage to know what is happening, which doesn't fully engage the audience and can limit scenes later. Also, since students have limited ability to think and show abstract skills, this is VERY hard for them.

TIPS FOR COACHING

Students should pick an easy sport and carefully pantomime each element. They should picture each piece of equipment and try to hold it the way one would in that actual sport, being sure to think about all aspects of the sport, such as how heavy the ball is, how you swing a bat, etc.

PREREQUISITE SKILLS

N/A

FUTURE SKILLS

Other pantomime games; more advanced scenes

DEBRIEF

Discuss with students that this is challenging but will become easier the more they do it and the slower they go (not slow motion; slightly slower than normal speed). Also, encourage students to practice pantomiming at home and think about how they can show what they are doing with an object that isn't really there. Let students share what was hardest about this activity.

IT LOOKS LIKE . . .

OVERARCHING SKILL

"Yes, and . . ."; pantomime

STRUCTURE OF ACTIVITY

One student is on stage and is joined by a second student after a short time. Together they create a scene. This can be done with two lines of students, one line on either side of the stage.

DURATION OF ACTIVITY

1–2 minutes per pair

EXPLANATION OF ACTIVITY

One student begins on stage pantomiming an activity, without explaining what they are doing. The second student enters and interprets what they are doing and then joins them in the scene. Whatever the second student guesses as the activity is officially the activity that the first student goes along with, even if it's not what they were initially showing.

EXAMPLE

A student might start pantomiming as if they are mowing the lawn. The second student enters and says, "Here, let me help you with your shopping cart. Looks like one of the wheels is wobbly." Even though that wasn't what the initial student was showing, they must then go along with the scene about the shopping cart.

PURPOSE OF ACTIVITY

This game forces students to practice using pantomime to start scenes and show their scene partner some information about the environment. Also, by letting the other person enter and introduce their spin on the pantomime, players are forced to be flexible and adjust their intentions as needed.

INTRODUCTORY MODIFICATIONS

Teachers can give the first student the activity to get started.

ADVANCED MODIFICATIONS

Have the first student justify the adjustment introduced by the second student.

PITFALLS

Students often respond with, "no, I'm doing. . . ." Remind them to use "yes, and . . ." and be flexible. The purpose is to adapt to the suggestions as the scene develops, not be stuck in their original idea.

TIPS FOR COACHING

Students should have fun with the fact that, often, what they pantomime can be seen in different ways. Make sure they slow down their mime work so that it is as clear as can be, and that they don't add other information (i.e., sound effects). Remind them that it is OK if their idea is interpreted differently.

PREREQUISITE SKILLS

Pantomime skills; basic scene work

FUTURE SKILLS

Advanced scenes and games (e.g., *Pan Left/Pan Right*, *Blind Line*, etc.)

DEBRIEF

Discuss with students which part of this game they liked more – starting the scene or entering the scene. Try to understand which part was easier for them, and why, so you can adjust teaching in the future. Revisit some moments that stood out as particularly good pantomime or scenes and discuss what made them work. As students become better at pantomime, see if others have greater success at correctly guessing what they were doing in the scene.

OBJECT SHARE

OVERARCHING SKILL

Pantomime; imitation

STRUCTURE OF ACTIVITY

Class split into pairs, either off stage or on stage.

DURATION OF ACTIVITY

5–10 minutes

EXPLANATION OF ACTIVITY

Students are split into pairs throughout the room. They decide on a physical object to use. The first student pantomimes using the object and then the second student takes the object from them and uses it in a slightly different way. They can pass the object back and forth, each taking turns using the object.

EXAMPLE

One student uses a hammer to hang a picture on the wall. The other student takes the hammer and uses it to finish building the bench that he was working on. They pass the hammer back and forth, each holding it the same way.

PURPOSE OF ACTIVITY

By seeing how someone else pantomimes using an object, students can practice seeing and interpreting that object but also discover how they will use the same object. Pantomime is very challenging for students so it is helpful for them to see it for themselves and then try to show what they just saw in their own way.

INTRODUCTORY MODIFICATIONS

Have students use the objects in the exact same way.

ADVANCED MODIFICATIONS

Turn the sharing of the object into a scene. Or have students not say what their object is and let the other person try to figure it out.

PITFALLS

Students go fast and show sloppy pantomiming, which makes it harder for others to see the specific movements and guess what they are trying to show. Encourage students to move slowly and make clear, decisive movements.

TIPS FOR COACHING

Ask the students if they are taking into account the weight, temperature, and texture of the object. Make sure they reflect in their movements how the object is really held rather than representing the cliche version of it (e.g., a phone is not usually held with the thumb and pinky finger).

PREREQUISITE SKILLS

Basic pantomime

FUTURE SKILLS

Advanced pantomime games

DEBRIEF

Pantomime can be a very challenging skill for many students. Encourage them to talk about what was easy but also what was hard about this. You might hear things like, "this just doesn't make sense," or even, "I don't understand this." That is OK. Remind students that you are practicing so you can see and show what is occurring in the made-up environment. This also brings life to the scene and adds color to the environment. Encourage students to take their time and point out that progression with this skill may come slowly, but that is OK – not everyone is great at pantomime, but they can still be great in scenes.

PANTOMIME SHOW AND TELL

OVERARCHING SKILL

Pantomime; audience presentation

STRUCTURE OF ACTIVITY

One student on stage in front of the class.

DURATION OF ACTIVITY

About 2–3 minutes per student

EXPLANATION OF ACTIVITY

One at a time, students step on the stage and show, through pantomime and dialogue, an object that they have brought to the class. They show all the details, holding the object as if it is actually there and explaining the specifics of it. Afterward, the class gets to ask two or three questions about it that the student answers.

EXAMPLE

A student might bring in his pet frog in an aquarium. He would mime putting the aquarium on the stage (a stool, downstage center is helpful for this game) and then taking the frog out in his palm and pointing out the size of his back legs, the warts on his face, his color, texture, and maybe showing the class how he can hop around the stage a bit. Perhaps it starts to hop away and the student has to retrieve it and then carefully pick it up again and place it back in the aquarium.

PURPOSE OF ACTIVITY

The purpose of this game is to help students describe an item as if it were actually there (including size, color, weight, and other details) and also interact with the object as if it were there (how it is held, what happens if it is dropped, if part of it moves). Additionally, this game is good practice being in front of an audience and talking to them in a fun and engaging manner.

INTRODUCTORY MODIFICATIONS

Give students an object that is simple to describe and interact with (e.g., pencil, hat, shoe). You may also need to have a picture or the actual object to help students for the first round.

ADVANCED MODIFICATIONS

Give objects that are harder to describe and have moving parts (e.g., skateboard, dental floss, scissors).

PITFALLS

Students will struggle with giving details about the object and interacting with it in the way you would if it was there. Are they holding it the right way and showing the attributes of the object? You may need to ask guiding questions to help them get started.

TIPS FOR COACHING

Make sure that students are aware of the weight, size, and texture of the object, as well as how fragile it might be and how they would actually hold it. Do they use just their fingers or their entire hand?

PREREQUISITE SKILLS

Basic pantomime skills

FUTURE SKILLS

Advanced pantomime games (e.g., *Slo-Mo*)

DEBRIEF

There are two aspects of this game to discuss during the debrief. The first is how the student felt being on stage in front of an audience. Was it easy to describe the item and how did it feel projecting their voice so everyone could hear? The second part is the pantomime piece. How did students hold the object and did that help them visualize what they were thinking or did it get in their way? Discuss as a group and see what worked for each individual.

TEACH AN ALIEN

OVERARCHING SKILL

Pantomime; gibberish

STRUCTURE OF ACTIVITY

Two people on stage in front of the class. This game can also be done in pairs throughout the room.

DURATION OF ACTIVITY

2–3 minutes per pair

EXPLANATION OF ACTIVITY

Two students step on stage. The teacher gives student B an activity but doesn't share what this activity is with Student A. Then using gibberish and panto-mime, Student B tries to teach and model the activity for Student A. Both students are only allowed to use gibberish.

EXAMPLE

The activity given to Student B might be making spaghetti.

Student B might start by bringing the Alien into their kitchen, miming taking out a pot, filling it with water, putting it on the stove, turning the stove on, and then waiting. Then they mime opening a cabinet, taking out a box, pouring the spaghetti into the pot (maybe breaking it in half first). Then, finally, taking one strand out and testing it by throwing it on the wall, etc.

PURPOSE OF ACTIVITY

Pantomime and gibberish are both very hard for our students but are great skills to have for scenes and future games. This game is designed specifically to prac-tice both of those things in a light and fun way, and to help develop pantomime and gibberish as foundation skills.

INTRODUCTORY MODIFICATIONS

N/A

ADVANCED MODIFICATIONS

N/A

PITFALLS

Students go very fast with their pantomime and can be very sloppy, which makes it hard for the audience to understand what they are doing. To help this skill develop, have students start with familiar activities and focus on moving clearly and slowly.

TIPS FOR COACHING

This game is all about communication, so both students need to dial in and focus on each other. If the "alien" character doesn't understand a step, they should let the other student know that they are confused or lost, all in gibberish. Students should also move slowly through the activity, making sure that every detail is illustrated and they do not skip any steps.

PREREQUISITE SKILLS

N/A

FUTURE SKILLS

Other pantomime games

DEBRIEF

This game is hard, but the element of teaching the activity to another student helps students understand the purpose a bit better. Ask students what stood out in terms of gibberish and pantomime and discuss highlights and challenges. Students will feel frustrated with this activity to start, but encourage them to practice at home or pay attention to simple activities like brushing teeth or taking out the trash. Then, the next time they try this they will likely show improvement.

TEACHER

OVERARCHING SKILL

Pantomime skills; explanation skills

STRUCTURE OF ACTIVITY

Students sit in a circle on the floor and describe activities to each other one at a time.

DURATION OF ACTIVITY

2–4 minutes per student

EXPLANATION OF ACTIVITY

Students sit in a circle on the floor. One at a time, a student will "teach" the rest of the circle how to do a simple task by demonstrating it through pantomime while describing each step in detail. The students being taught act out each step along with the person doing the demonstration.

EXAMPLE

A student might tell the class that they are teaching how to make a peanut butter and jelly sandwich. They might say, "First, I take out the bread from the refrigerator," while miming opening the fridge, reaching in, and taking out a loaf of bread. "Then I remove the bread from the package" (while miming this action). "I open the cupboard and take out the jar of peanut butter and unscrew it," etc.

PURPOSE OF ACTIVITY

Practicing pantomime makes our students better performers because it helps their scenes and performances come to life. This game will help teach them how to show each movement deliberately and how to make each action clear.

INTRODUCTORY MODIFICATIONS

Have students start with a very easy task or show part of the task yourself. It is also possible for students to narrate the activities of the teacher while the teacher models the gestures and everyone follows along.

ADVANCED MODIFICATIONS

Have students perform the actions without describing (or even talking about something else) and see if others can imitate and guess what they are demonstrating.

PITFALLS

Pantomime is challenging for our students and they tend to rush through and show sloppy gestures. Remind them to slow down and really describe what they would be doing as if it were real. The description will help them visualize and imagine the next steps, making their pantomime work more believable.

TIPS FOR COACHING

The slower a student goes, the more they will be able to see the detail. They need to try to clearly see the objects, what they feel like, how heavy they are, etc., and carefully go through each detail.

PREREQUISITE SKILLS

N/A

FUTURE SKILLS

Advanced scene games; other pantomime games

DEBRIEF

This skill set is very challenging for our students. Ask students if the explaining part made things easier for them to visualize and perform each step. Encourage them to practice outside of class and observe how they perform normal daily routines at home (brushing teeth, washing the dog, making a sandwich). Have students talk about what makes pantomime hard and how practice can help them improve. Remind them that even a little improvement goes a long way.

WHERE ARE YOU?

OVERARCHING SKILL

Pantomime

STRUCTURE OF ACTIVITY

One student alone on stage.

DURATION OF ACTIVITY

About 30 seconds per student

EXPLANATION OF ACTIVITY

Students step on stage one at a time and mime being in a location. They stay on stage for approximately 30 seconds, adding detail to their location until the class guesses where they are.

EXAMPLE

A student might mime walking through an automatic door, pulling out a shopping cart, walking down an aisle, looking at products, putting them in the cart, then finally checking out and paying. Each moment is carefully pantomimed, as if they were really carrying out the actions within the locations.

PURPOSE OF ACTIVITY

To encourage students to slow down and show very pronounced pantomime. By interacting with the space and using it, they can give the audience and other students a clear vision of what they see. But, they have to show with some precision what they are seeing or it is left for the audience to guess (which leads to confusion and pulls away from the scene).

INTRODUCTORY MODIFICATIONS

If needed, students can narrate what they are doing or speak as they normally would in that space (without saying where they are).

ADVANCED MODIFICATIONS

N/A

PITFALLS

Students tend to rush through their pantomime and it doesn't give a vision to anyone except themselves. Work with them to slow them down and ensure they really demonstrate each step so that it is obvious to anyone in the audience. This is extremely hard for our students and may push their frustrations.

TIPS FOR COACHING

It is easy for students to cut corners and not actually include all the elements, meaning they may run out of things to mime. Tell the students to visualize what they would actually be seeing in front of them and to take their time, using each element in the way that they would actually be used.

PREREQUISITE SKILLS

Intro pantomime

FUTURE SKILLS

Advanced pantomime and scenes (e.g., *Silent Tension*)

DEBRIEF

Students have a hard time with this skill, so check in on their frustration levels. This game is challenging for many and should be introduced slowly, without other challenging games alongside it. Check in with students to highlight great moments and discuss what felt good and what worked. Try to avoid any criticism for the first few practices of this game to keep feelings positive. Have students share what they learned and how they felt working in their space.

CHARACTER GAMES

One of the most popular concepts in improvised theatre is for students to create new characters that are introduced within scenes and improv games. Since every scene develops from a new idea, there are unlimited choices for a student to make each time.

Character work can be both frightening and exciting for students, since it asks them to step outside of themselves and to look at ideas from a new perspective. There are numerous ways to explore character work, and there are a great many exercises that focus on this.

Specifically, a recognizable character has a point of view, a background, and a way of talking, moving, and behaving. In improvised theatre, there is very little time to invent a character, so actors need to make very quick decisions and fill in the gaps as a scene progresses.

An actor, for example, might begin a scene as an old woman with a walker, but as the scene progresses, we might find out that she is a retired spy and has inside knowledge of the world of espionage. It might be complicated by her limited movement, but it would be fun to watch the struggle and how it is incorporated into the scene, and it allows us to see additional layers to a character.

Very often, a character can be immediately discovered based on the situation or occupation. As an exercise, assigning an unlikely description before an occupation can provide clues as to how the character talks and how they see the world. For example, a forgetful dentist or an enthusiastic fireman. Each of these suggestions provides easy ideas to the performer as to possible directions they could take in the personification of that character.

Characters also provide the opportunity for a performer to bring in their own voice or point of view but to have it personified by a separate entity. The idea of playing a sinister character that speaks to the darker part of the performer's own life can be very cathartic and lead to a more honest portrayal.

Above all, characters should be played as real as possible rather than just for cheap laughs (unless that is the intent). The more a character is based on realism, the more recognizable it is for the audience and the more impactful it will be. It's always best practice to encourage the performers to find the "truth" of a character and to play that, and just to let the dialogue flow from how the character is speaking rather than trying to come up with the funniest line.

ANIMAL CLUE

OVERARCHING SKILL

Giving subtle clues while being on stage by yourself

STRUCTURE OF ACTIVITY

One student stands on stage and presents a short monologue, delivered from the perspective of an animal. They then field questions about their animal until the other students guess what the animal is.

DURATION OF ACTIVITY

20 minutes

EXPLANATION OF ACTIVITY

One student steps on stage and the teacher either whispers the name of an animal to them or they come up with their own idea. They then present a short monologue, as if they were the animal speaking, incorporating characteristics of the animal itself (e.g., a donkey might speak slowly). They don't act like the animal, they just give subtle clues as to what they are. They then field questions from the audience about themselves until the audience can guess the animal.

EXAMPLE

A student may say, speaking with a deep, slow voice, "Hello, it's nice to *meet* you. It's been kind of tough for me lately because I found out I'm lactose intolerant. Everyone's been making fun of me, but I think I'm going to *milk* this for more sympathy. I'm concerned that I might have to get an *udder* job. . . ."

PURPOSE OF ACTIVITY

Being on stage in front of people can be challenging. The purpose of this game is to help students feel comfortable being on stage while they practice giving the audience clues that are not too obvious. They can also work on building puns into their monologue and answering questions on the spot.

INTRODUCTORY MODIFICATIONS

The teacher could give students the animal and could also be on stage with the student and help them answer questions to get students started.

ADVANCED MODIFICATIONS

You can give students the opportunity to present in pairs. This allows them to try building off each other's clues.

PITFALLS

Often students give the most obvious clues first or say the animal that they are trying to be. Work to come up with more clues and be less obvious over time.

TIPS FOR COACHING

It is helpful to remind students about what motivates the animal. They can give clues about what they like to eat or where they live without giving too much away. Their goal is to keep the audience guessing and trying to figure out the animal they are trying to emulate.

PREREQUISITE SKILLS

N/A

FUTURE SKILLS

By understanding what motivates various animals, students can develop characters in scenes or adjust how they interact with the environment; *Horse Meets Pig*

DEBRIEF

Talk to students about how it felt to be in front of the audience and how it felt to answer questions. It is good for them to recognize that as a skill set and learn that overcoming stage fright will help them in other ways in the future. Also, discuss what worked and what didn't, both for answering questions and giving clues. It can be hard to answer questions on the spot, so praise their effort.

BRUNCH WITH . . .

OVERARCHING SKILL

Character development; perspective taking

STRUCTURE OF ACTIVITY

Students sit in a circle in groups of three or four.

DURATION OF ACTIVITY

5 minutes per group

EXPLANATION OF ACTIVITY

Students sit in a small group with three to four people in a circle and each person is assigned a character or famous person. They then have "brunch" together and talk about life, or any subject, staying in character throughout and offering their insights based on their character's perspective.

EXAMPLE

Three students – one is Alexander Hamilton, one is a pirate, and one is a dinosaur. They start discussing the bill from brunch – the Hamilton character might mention the financial implication of paying the bill, the pirate might talk about how he has a treasure chest that could cover the total amount, if only they could find the map, and the dinosaur might not be able to reach the bill because his arms are too short. We see how their different perspectives can change what the main concerns of their characters are.

PURPOSE OF ACTIVITY

When you sit down to have brunch with someone you talk about more than just the restaurant. What else would a character have concerns about? This is an opportunity to explore playing another character while maintaining a conversation, sharing insight, discussing struggles that person might face, and giving advice from that person's perspective.

INTRODUCTORY MODIFICATIONS

You could begin by doing this game in pairs, with just two people sitting face to face and taking on familiar characters. See if they can keep the conversation going for a couple minutes.

ADVANCED MODIFICATIONS

Have members of the group be from different time periods, stories, or genres. You can also have the students not know the other students' perspectives and have to guess who they were pretending to be at the end.

PITFALLS

Many students will say who they are up front and not have an existing relationship with their stage partner. Try to avoid the introduction scene. Also, students will get stuck talking about the restaurant or the brunch instead of what might be happening in their regular daily routines or lives. Work to shift their thinking out of the immediate time and place.

TIPS FOR COACHING

Students do not need to do impersonations of the characters. They can play them close to their "normal" tone of voice. What we want to see is what the characters are thinking and how their background and circumstances affect their dialogue.

PREREQUISITE SKILLS

Basic scene work; character creation

FUTURE SKILLS

Advanced scenes; character games

DEBRIEF

Check in with players to see what worked in the scene and what they discussed. Encourage them to have broad conversations and not be tied to the location or brunch. Have them think about what that character is motivated by/worried about/limited by outside of that immediate time and place.

BUS STOP

OVERARCHING SKILL

Character development; introductory scene work

STRUCTURE OF ACTIVITY

One or two people sitting on a bench. Periodically a new student will enter from one side and everyone slides over on the bench, with the end person on the other side then exiting the scene.

DURATION OF ACTIVITY

10 minutes

EXPLANATION OF ACTIVITY

One student (or two for more advanced groups) starts by sitting on a bench on the stage, which represents a bus stop. A new student enters the scene and sits next to them. This new student has a specific characteristic about them (e.g., they're very old, they have an accent, etc.). The first student has to figure out what is different about them and then take on the same characteristics, so they become the same type of character. After about 30 seconds of conversation a new student enters and the original student exits to catch their bus, typically mentioning where they're going. The new student has a different characteristic and the process repeats.

EXAMPLE

Student A is on the bench. Student B enters and does three push-ups and then sits down. Student A says hello and Student B answers with a tough guy voice while flexing and staring at his muscles. Student A recognizes what B is doing and also starts doing stretching exercises while discussing when the bus might be arriving. This continues until Student C arrives. Student A then leaves to catch their bus and Student C might say, "Live long and prosper," and show B the vulcan hand salute, etc.

PURPOSE OF ACTIVITY

This game forces students to make strong, easily identifiable character choices (motivation, body postures, movements, voice, etc.). This allows for other students to do their best interpretation of that character and show those same attributes in their own way.

INTRODUCTORY MODIFICATIONS

Start with one student on stage and introduce one at a time. Also, pre-identify several characters that can be chosen. You may need to help newer students pick a character to get started.

ADVANCED MODIFICATIONS

Have students be a little more subtle with their characters. This is also a good chance to build the idea of differences in character status into some of these scenes.

PITFALLS

Students tend to default to being themselves or play a very subtle version of the character they are portraying. Some students also dominate the conversation and don't allow for others to share the stage and drive the scene. When exiting, try to have them justify why they are getting on the bus (e.g., "Here is my bus, I'm off to work").

TIPS FOR COACHING

Coach students to play up or down their character attributes. Encourage students to take on a more pronounced version of each character.

PREREQUISITE SKILLS

N/A

FUTURE SKILLS

Advanced character skills in scene work

DEBRIEF

Talk to students about which was harder – creating their own character or imitating someone else's. Discuss what made it easier to do each of these things and what worked/didn't work in the scene exchange. Try to get them to understand that the more clearly they show an attribute, the easier it will be for the audience and their stage partners to see, which will help drive a scene. Also discuss the concepts of gifts during this game (someone identifying a key characteristic to help define your character).

CHARACTER DAY

OVERARCHING SKILL

Character development; "yes and . . ." in a newly established universe

STRUCTURE OF ACTIVITY

One student is assigned a character and then plays a succession of scenes.

DURATION OF ACTIVITY

15 minutes

EXPLANATION OF ACTIVITY

The class creates a character by listing all the qualities of that person. They come up with the character's name, what they do, what their interests are, what a typical day involves for them, their favorite activity, etc. One student is then assigned to play that character. We see the character begin the day and perhaps interact with another student at a location chosen by the teacher. At any point, the teacher can call out a new location and time, with the scene suddenly shifting there, and we see the same character interacting with new people in the new location.

EXAMPLE

The class might come up with a character named Alex. Alex is a software designer who likes to play Dungeons and Dragons. He also enjoys renaissance fairs and pretending to be a knight. Alex has a long beard and owns several cats.

In the first scene, we see Alex bored at work and acting much smarter than his boss. His boss asks him what he's doing over the weekend, and Alex replies that he's fighting in a role-playing battle on Saturday.

At this point, the teacher might call out, "let's see the battle scene." We then jump to another player portraying the biggest, meanest knight at the competition, with Alex having to face him. They start to play out that scene, in which Alex recognizes the big knight and realizes how scary he is. He tries to reason with him, but the bigger knight isn't happy about how Alex had treated him the previous month in their online role-playing game. The teacher might then call out, "we now shift to the hospital," and we might see Alex in a hospital bed playing D&D on his computer screen with his friends and explaining how he had almost beaten the knight, etc.

PURPOSE OF ACTIVITY

Showing all the different aspects of the character's day will help you learn more about that character and about their life. If you have that story in mind you will be able to switch characters more easily and portray someone else on stage (instead of yourself). Also, this allows for other characters to be developed around this one person to show their whole universe and really tell the story of their life.

INTRODUCTORY MODIFICATIONS

Assign characters from the beginning to allow people to think about their characters before being in the scene.

ADVANCED MODIFICATIONS

Teach students to do the "cut to" and allow them to run the game independently.

PITFALLS

Students who are learning this game might not know how to really start or end each scene, or recognise when a "gift" comes up in a scene. Often these gifts or clues can be secretive but open up a whole new dynamic for that character or that reality. Additionally, many of the scenes will start with characters saying "Hi" or making a statement about where they are (e.g., "It is so nice to see my doctor at the doctor's office").

TIPS FOR COACHING

Students should play the characters as realistically as possible without overly exaggerating their qualities. They are really looking for what makes the characters tick rather than going for the obvious jokes.

PREREQUISITE SKILLS

Character development; scene skills

FUTURE SKILLS

Long-form or montage-style games; advanced character games

DEBRIEF

For those that stayed as one character for all the scenes, discuss what they liked and disliked about that aspect of the game. For those that played other people, or were not the main character, discuss what they liked or disliked about their role in the game. Revisit conversations with students about how sometimes you are the main character and other times you are supplementing the scenes. If you are not the main character, don't try to hog the entire discussion but allow for the main character to react and develop so we can come back to them later in other scenarios.

CHARACTER WALK

OVERARCHING SKILL

Detailed creation of characters

STRUCTURE OF ACTIVITY

Students walk around the room with the teacher calling out different circumstances and side coaching.

DURATION OF ACTIVITY

5–10 minutes

EXPLANATION OF ACTIVITY

Each student comes up with a character (e.g., soldier, acrobat, chef) and begins to walk around the room, without talking, as that character would walk. Periodically, the teacher calls out more information – How does the character walk and why? How do they greet people? What is their attitude? Eventually, the teacher will call out different situations (e.g., it's raining, it's very hot, you're in a crowded train) and the students then react accordingly to this new information. At the end, students reveal who their character was and gives some background information about them.

EXAMPLE

N/A

PURPOSE OF ACTIVITY

As you are moving around you create a backstory for your character and a history that explains why they think and believe what they think and believe. This will help with later games as you learn to define your characters better, but for now, the purpose is to dive into one character and try to embody all that they are.

INTRODUCTORY MODIFICATIONS

Use characters that students are familiar with or discuss characters ahead of time.

ADVANCED MODIFICATIONS

Increase the interaction between characters. You can also add in a Q&A session at the end for each character or put the characters into scenes.

PITFALLS

Students will likely pick their favorite character from a movie or video game and get stuck on trying to portray them accurately instead of creating something of their own.

TIPS FOR COACHING

Ask students to create familiar types of people and to try to understand how they might think. How does a policeman approach a new person differently from how a minister would?

PREREQUISITE SKILLS

N/A

FUTURE SKILLS

Character games

DEBRIEF

Afterwards, discuss how they felt as a character and what influenced their decisions. Also, discuss what was easy and what felt hard for them with regard to this game. Many students get stuck not knowing the right answer to a question. In this class we have an opportunity to create the right answer. You can also talk about whether they liked their character or not. Sometimes we create characters that we don't like but it is OK to portray them on stage and then move on.

FAMILY MEMBER

OVERARCHING SKILL

Character development

STRUCTURE OF ACTIVITY

Two to three students in groups.

DURATION OF ACTIVITY

About 10 minutes

EXPLANATION OF ACTIVITY

Students are put in groups of two to three people. Each person portrays one of their family members while interacting with others in their group and reacting in the way they envision their family member would behave.

EXAMPLE

One student is playing their grandfather, the other their sister, and the third their dad. The grandfather character starts out having trouble using their cell phone, the sister character tells them that they are pretty good at tech and shows him how to use it. The dad character then asks if he can borrow the phone for a minute to watch the ballgame, etc. We might see the characters in some sort of conflict or getting along.

PURPOSE OF ACTIVITY

To use theory of mind as a skill to accurately portray someone else from your family. How does the family member think, act, walk, talk, etc.? If you can portray all of that with some accuracy, then you will be able to be that character on stage. Remember to consider the way they think and their motivation, and bring those driving factors into the scene.

INTRODUCTORY MODIFICATIONS

Teachers may need to help create the scene by giving students a family member to portray.

ADVANCED MODIFICATIONS

Have students pick another character from their family that they don't know as well and fill in the blanks with their own thoughts about what that character would do.

PITFALLS

Students tend to show the most extreme example of what that character can be like. If you are showing grandma, chances are she is not going to be throwing pretzels at the dog. Work to have students show accurate portrayals of characters and not wacky renditions.

TIPS FOR COACHING

Students should not be trying to do impersonations. They instead should work to capture how the person actually behaves, what their interests are, and how they typically react to things.

PREREQUISITE SKILLS

Basic character development

FUTURE SKILLS

Advanced character games and scenes

DEBRIEF

When debriefing, start by discussing what they liked about other students' portrayals and how they showed their family members. Then have them discuss what they showed in their own portrayals that could have given clues about this person, or how they tried to embody some of the characteristics of their chosen family member.

GOOD/BAD ADVICE

OVERARCHING SKILL

Quick thinking; detailed answers; being on stage in front of an audience

STRUCTURE OF ACTIVITY

Three students sit in chairs, side by side, facing the audience. They field questions from the audience and answer with varying degrees of good or bad advice.

DURATION OF ACTIVITY

10–15 minutes (small groups answer three to four questions each)

EXPLANATION OF ACTIVITY

Three students sit side by side on stage. The teacher has them introduce themselves and they all present a fictitious name and some details about their character. The teacher then asks for questions from the audience in which they are seeking advice. The first player provides good advice, the second player provides somewhat sketchy advice, and the third player provides terrible advice. Each group answers three to four questions from the audience.

EXAMPLE

First player (Samantha): "Hi, my name is Samantha and I'm a guidance counselor at Westmont Middle School."

Second player (Henry): "Hi, I'm Henry and I'm a cab driver."

Third player (Sunshine): "Hi. My name is Sunshine and I'm at peace with nature."

First question: My neighbor above me makes so much noise when they walk around. What do I do?

Samantha: "You should find out from them why they walk so loudly. Perhaps they are lonely and need a friend. Be their friend."

Henry: "I keep a baseball bat under my seat in case someone tries to rob me. I would take that bat and bang it into the ceiling every time they take a step."

Sunshine: "I have found that crystals have a calming effect on sound waves. I'm selling my new collection on my Etsy store and I can get you the details after the show. . . ."

PURPOSE OF ACTIVITY

To answer questions on topic and with details using a character's perspective, and strengthening students' ability to be on stage in front of an audience for longer time periods.

INTRODUCTORY MODIFICATIONS

This game can be simplified to include only two students, with one giving good advice and one giving bad advice. That helps for some students who struggle with the intermediary answers. You can also leave out the character aspect of this game to start.

ADVANCED MODIFICATIONS

The three chairs can be changed from good/medium/bad advice to good/bad/worst advice. Also, it is good to add in character depth when possible.

PITFALLS

Students often struggle to give bad advice that is on topic (they either default to good advice or go far too extreme). Also, when building on the character aspect of this, they answer the question from their own perspective, not that of the character's.

TIPS FOR COACHING

Make sure that you have a discussion ahead of time about what is appropriate and what isn't. Some students will be more comfortable giving really bad advice than others. It's a good idea to make sure everyone is on the same page and respecting the audience and other students.

PREREQUISITE SKILLS

N/A

FUTURE SKILLS

Other more advanced Q&A games

DEBRIEF

Don't spend too much time on the debrief of this game in terms of the advice given. Instead, focus more on the delivery of answers with confidence, with detail, and at an appropriate volume. These are skills that transcend this game but can be emphasized here in a fun and engaging way. Also, these skills will be pivotal when adding in other advanced games and in setting a foundation for future performances.

HORSE MEETS PIG

OVERARCHING SKILL

Practicing theory of mind by taking on characteristics of an animal and using that in a scene

STRUCTURE OF ACTIVITY

Two students on stage, each representing an animal, creating a short scene.

DURATION OF ACTIVITY

10–15 minutes

EXPLANATION OF ACTIVITY

Based on the game *Animal Clue*, two students will each play an animal. Two different "animals" meet, each speaking English and walking as humans while having a conversation. The students do not reveal which animals they are playing until the end of the game, after their scene partner guesses what they are.

EXAMPLE

Two students create a scene at a coffee shop. One licks the back of his hands and washes his face with them before sitting down. The other walks in a tight circle, several times, before sitting.

Student One: It's ironic that we're meeting, most people would think we hate each other.

Student Two: Yeah, but it was nice of you to bring me that ball. I had hours of fun with it.

Student One: Really? I think I napped 18 hours today. I was on the bed, then on the shelf, then I spent the rest of the evening hiding in the closet. It was great.

Student Two: You really should get outside more. I have a whole yard to run around in. It's filled with sticks, which are super fun.

Student One: I'm more of an indoors type. But yesterday, my owner shined a flashlight on the ground and I chased it for almost 30 seconds before I got bored . . .

PURPOSE OF ACTIVITY

To work on character development by practicing taking on different characteristics of animals. Animals have different motivations, including food preferences, living arrangements, etc. If they use that motivation in a scene with someone else, they are more likely to have a quality scene with conflict and varied interactions.

INTRODUCTORY MODIFICATIONS

Keep the location easy and familiar to start.

ADVANCED MODIFICATIONS

Change locations and include conflicts to build a quality scene.

PITFALLS

If you are pretending to be an animal, you don't say you are that animal. Many students will label the animal they are attempting to portray on stage. Instead of that, they can give clues, make puns, or make decisions based on that animal's motivations. The audience doesn't need to know what type of animal they're pretending to be, they just need to see a character make consistent decisions.

TIPS FOR COACHING

Encourage students to make every decision as if they were that animal – from how they stand, to how they talk, to what they talk about, to what they do. All of that should be influenced by the animal they are trying to portray.

PREREQUISITE SKILLS

Animal Clue; general scene work

FUTURE SKILLS

Other scene work or character games

DEBRIEF

Focus on their scene as that animal as a whole instead of specifically on their portrayal of the actual animal. This is really a scene game with the animal being an idea generator. Remind them to focus on quality scene work and not get stuck on the gimmick of being an animal.

I AM

OVERARCHING SKILL

Listening; giving clues in a conversation

STRUCTURE OF ACTIVITY

Students sitting and having a discussion in pairs.

DURATION OF ACTIVITY

5 minutes

EXPLANATION OF ACTIVITY

Students are paired up around the room. Each student thinks of an occupation, without telling the other, and they have a short conversation about their day or week. The students will give subtle clues as to what their occupation is, without actually telling their scene partner. At the end of a couple of minutes, each student tries to guess the other's occupation.

EXAMPLE

One student is a pilot and the other is a fireman. They are discussing their week and the fireman says it's been busy and he can't get the ringing out of his head. The pilot agrees, saying he feels like he's been all over the place and never seems to sleep at home, etc. The fireman asks if the pilot has an escape plan for his home, and the pilot answers that he always does a pre-check before everything he does, etc.

PURPOSE OF ACTIVITY

To use your understanding of a job to give clues about what your stresses and successes may be while you are also listening and decoding clues from your partner.

INTRODUCTORY MODIFICATIONS

You could start with both parties knowing the other person's job. This will make the conversation easier and a bit more fluid. One person can also play themselves while the other gives clues.

ADVANCED MODIFICATIONS

N/A

PITFALLS

Many students will open the conversation by saying their occupation (e.g., I am a pilot). This isn't how a typical conversation would go and it takes the fun out of the guessing part of the game.

TIPS FOR COACHING

Students should talk about what life is like for them with the occupation they have without revealing too many specifics about what they do. Teachers don't always just talk about teaching, for example, they might discuss the commute, budget cuts, etc.

PREREQUISITE SKILLS

Basic character games; other interview games

FUTURE SKILLS

More advanced clue giving games; other interview formats

DEBRIEF

When debriefing, discuss what worked and what didn't when giving clues. Also talk about how they figured out what job the other person had and what questions they used to reach their conclusion. The underlying purpose of this game is to ask quality questions, so discuss which questions they asked that were helpful and which ones didn't result in good information.

IF I WERE A SPOON

OVERARCHING SKILL

Character portrayal in scenes

STRUCTURE OF ACTIVITY

Two students on stage creating a short scene.

DURATION OF ACTIVITY

2–3 minutes per group

EXPLANATION OF ACTIVITY

Each student is assigned a different inanimate object. Each pair then acts out a short scene, with each student acting as if they are their designated object, with all the concerns, emotions, and conflicts that the object might have. The audience then guess what objects each student is.

EXAMPLE

One student is a lightbulb and the other is a locomotive. They meet and the lightbulb mentions that she misses seeing the world and only gets to be seen at night. The locomotive understands and mentions that he is so tired after climbing up and down hills all day, and has been lonely since he's always in front of everybody. They realize that perhaps they could work together and spend time in each other's company. The locomotive says that he needs a new light in his nose, so they join forces and travel the country together.

PURPOSE OF ACTIVITY

To think about how the world looks from another person's perspective, which is a key skill in improv and in this game. By knowing what the inanimate object does you will have an idea of what they are good at, what upsets them, what drives their decision making, etc. This also helps you view the world from their perspective, making you better connected.

INTRODUCTORY MODIFICATIONS

You can have both people know what object the other person is demonstrating.

ADVANCED MODIFICATIONS

N/A

PITFALLS

Students often want to just say what they are or be very obvious with their clues. Work to have them be subtle but also clear and decisive with their objects' opinions.

TIPS FOR COACHING

Students should try not to say what they actually are but rather how they are feeling about who they are.

PREREQUISITE SKILLS

N/A

FUTURE SKILLS

More advanced character scenes and games

DEBRIEF

When discussing this game, ask students how they decided their object's attitude and viewpoint of the world. A spoon could be very happy to be a spoon or really despise being a spoon, but either way, they will have an opinion about it. Also, discuss how all the characters would be if they were put into different locations (e.g., a spoon would love being at a dinner table but hate being in the trash; a garbage bag would hate being at a dinner table but love being in the trash).

JOB INTERVIEW

OVERARCHING SKILL

Making up questions and answers

STRUCTURE OF ACTIVITY

Students working in pairs with multiple pairs working at once.

DURATION OF ACTIVITY

5–10 minutes

EXPLANATION OF ACTIVITY

Teacher suggests a job. One student will then be in a mock interview for that job, acting as an expert, while the other interviews them. After the job interview is completed, the teacher gives a new job suggestion and the students reverse roles.

EXAMPLE

The suggestion is submarine captain.

Student 1: "I'm here for the job as sub captain."

Student 2: "I've looked over your resume and you seem well qualified."

Student 1: "Yes, I've worked on 4 different types of subs, both nuclear and conventional. I was also a chief periscope polisher for 6 months and was even fired out as a test torpedo."

Student 2: "How good are you at being underwater for long periods of time?"

Student 1: "Well, I'm not a big fan of baths or swimming pools, but if there's a huge amount of metal around me, I'm pretty good."

Student 2: "We spend a lot of time in cramped quarters here, is that an issue?"

Student 1: "I had six brothers and seven sisters, and we grew up in a one bedroom apartment in Manhattan. Does that answer your question?"

PURPOSE OF ACTIVITY

By pretending that both people are experts, they are required to come up with questions and answers that are content-specific and that they would both know the answers to. They also have to practice "Yes, and . . ." by working together to create a new alternate reality.

INTRODUCTORY MODIFICATIONS

The topic could start as a familiar one to get started. You could also do this in small groups so no one person is coming up with too much information on their own.

ADVANCED MODIFICATION

Let each group of students come up with their own expertise and suggestion for the job.

PITFALLS

Students tend to answer questions without any detail because they are worried about being wrong or not knowing the answer. Encourage them to throw in details even if they are made up so that it will give more credibility to their character.

TIPS FOR COACHING

Students should speak with confidence and think about all the specifics that they might know, or have heard, about the given profession. The more specifics they add, the more they sound like they know what they are doing.

PREREQUISITE SKILLS

Basic character and scene work

FUTURE SKILLS

Advanced interview games (e.g., *Expert*); other clue-giving games

DEBRIEF

Discuss which was easier – asking the questions or giving the answers. Talk about how good questions are open ended and allow for some creativity from their partners. Also talk about whether the person would've been given the job and why.

INTRO-VIEW

OVERARCHING SKILL

Creating a backstory for a character and presenting that to an audience

STRUCTURE OF ACTIVITY

One person on stage, fielding questions from the class after a brief monologue.

DURATION OF ACTIVITY

3–5 minutes per person

EXPLANATION OF ACTIVITY

To begin, a student will introduce him/herself in front of the class. They will say their name, where they are from, and perhaps a hobby or two. The class will then ask questions so that the student can expand on their intro. Second time around, students will introduce themselves as a new character and repeat the process.

EXAMPLE

A student might say, "Hi, my name is Dennis Ploesch, and I'm a plumber. I like collecting stamps and I live in Canada. I'm originally from Florida, but I've lived in Canada for the past 5 years." The students might ask about his stamp collection, what it's like to be a plumber in a cold climate, what the hardest part of his job is, why he moved from Florida, whether he speaks French, etc.

PURPOSE OF ACTIVITY

Having a backstory to your character will give them depth and allow them to make unique decisions. It also helps students understand other people's perspectives, which can help them relate socially to peers.

INTRODUCTORY MODIFICATIONS

Have them play this as themselves for the first round. This will help set up the structure of the game and get them comfortable with the format.

ADVANCED MODIFICATIONS

For those who are good at creating a backstory for individual characters, have them work in pairs to create a backstory for each other. They can discuss how they met, what type of relationship they have currently, what they fight about, etc.

PITFALLS

Students often give vague answers to questions or respond with some form of "I don't know." Push them to give a specific answer and remind them that any answer they give is the correct answer. When you are a character, you know everything there is to know about him/her.

TIPS FOR COACHING

Have students consider how their backstory helps to define who they are and their answers to the questions. They shouldn't try to give long, complicated answers to the questions, but rather realistic ones based on their background and experience.

PREREQUISITE SKILLS

Basic character skills

FUTURE SKILLS

This game helps with creating characters for *Good/Bad Advice*, general character scenes, and other interview/clue-giving games

DEBRIEF

When discussing with students, make sure to highlight that the more detail they give, the easier the conversation will be. Remind them that any answer they give is the right answer but try to keep them on topic and relatable. Also ask students which was easier, the monologue or the answering of questions? Discuss why it may be easier to answer a question than to come up with a whole monologue and how that can relate to scene work later.

MEET YOURSELF

OVERARCHING SKILL

Character development; "yes and . . ."

STRUCTURE OF ACTIVITY

Student stands on stage and does a monologue based on information given to them.

DURATION OF ACTIVITY

2–3 minutes per student

EXPLANATION OF ACTIVITY

Each person in the class gets three slips of paper. On one of the pieces of paper they each write down the name of a character, on another an age, and on the final piece of paper an occupation. The pieces of paper are then all collected with others of the same category and each category is mixed up. One at a time, a student draws from each pile. They then step in front of the class and introduce themselves, and tell a little about their day or their point of view on life in general.

EXAMPLE

A student might draw that they are a plumber, they are 59 years old, and their name is Alistair. They could speak in a rich-sounding voice, describe how their work has social implications, and maybe lament the fact that the other plumbers don't respect them because they don't seem to fit in or get their jokes.

PURPOSE OF ACTIVITY

Becoming a character and knowing everything there is about them is a challenge. But practicing giving an answer with confidence on stage is a great skill for public speaking and being confident in talking to others. This will help as an improviser and in general life.

INTRODUCTORY MODIFICATIONS

It may be good to give some individuals their three pieces of paper with the suggestions on early so they have time to think and process who that character might be before speaking in front of the class.

ADVANCED MODIFICATIONS

Give the students a fourth piece of paper with something that just happened on it (e.g., just lost his wallet; just got a parking ticket; just got fired).

PITFALLS

Students tend to bring themselves into their characters or not know how to answer questions. Remind them that any answer they give is the correct answer and nobody will know that character the way they do.

TIPS FOR COACHING

Students can build how a character talks and their point of view based on simple details, such as name, occupation, and age. How much experience does this person have and do they like their job?

PREREQUISITE SKILLS

N/A

FUTURE SKILLS

Advanced character games and scenes

DEBRIEF

Discuss what was the hardest/easiest aspect of their character to show on stage. Also discuss what clues came from their answers to previous questions and how they showed that in future responses (e.g., if the character was very forgetful, how did they show that in other ways in other questions). Also, talk to students about how they can be those characters in scenes and know their entire backstory without having to share the entire backstory each time.

NOT-TRODUCTION

OVERARCHING SKILL

Quick creative thinking

STRUCTURE OF ACTIVITY

One student at a time on stage.

DURATION OF ACTIVITY

2–3 minutes per student

EXPLANATION OF ACTIVITY

A student steps on stage and introduces themself with misinformation. They say four to five things about themselves that are absolutely not true. The class then asks a series of rapid-fire questions, which the student must answer as the character they just created.

EXAMPLE

A student might stand on stage and say, "Hi, my name is Richie Mussina and I am 6'2" tall and I'm a jockey. I'm from Paris originally and I've been married 6 times." The class might then ask questions about what it's like to be a tall jockey, why he's been married so many times, if he has problems with the English language, etc.

PURPOSE OF ACTIVITY

Many students get stuck on being right all the time and they are afraid to take chances. In this game, the entire purpose is to be wrong, so students are safe to take a chance. This game also forces students to think quickly and be creative in their answers. Any answer they give here is OK (as long as it is appropriate).

INTRODUCTORY MODIFICATIONS

You could give students a set list of things to share (e.g., name, age, where they live, etc.).

ADVANCED MODIFICATIONS

N/A

PITFALLS

Students can get stuck thinking. Work to have them respond quickly and give answers that are wrong as fast as they can. If someone asks your favorite color, don't worry about giving the right answer or analyzing which color is your favorite – say the first color that comes to mind (as long as it isn't their real favorite color). This encourages students to be flexible and explorative in their answers.

TIPS FOR COACHING

Everything the student comes up with is correct and they should answer the questions quickly, without being too concerned about whether their answers exactly match the information they previously gave. Encourage them to not think too much about giving the "right" answer. Also, students may come up with overly "wacky" ideas for their character. Have them ground their answers in some sense of reality to make it easier to play.

PREREQUISITE SKILLS

Basic character; "yes, and . . ."

FUTURE SKILLS

More complex character games (e.g., *Expert, Job Interview*)

DEBRIEF

Ask students if it was hard to make up answers about themselves. Discuss how what they did was not just create a new character but play a variation of themselves, which can then be used as a character in scenes or other games.

ONE SUGGESTION CHARACTER

OVERARCHING SKILL

Character generating; point of view

STRUCTURE OF ACTIVITY

Teacher gets the class to brainstorm together, then students get in pairs throughout the room.

DURATION OF ACTIVITY

10 minutes

EXPLANATION OF ACTIVITY

Teacher stands in front of the room and gets the suggestion of a location from the class. The class then starts to brainstorm all the types of people who might populate that location as the teacher writes them on a whiteboard. Students are then split into pairs, with each student taking one of the characters and having a brief discussion/scene with their scene partner as that character. After a couple of minutes, the students all switch partners and repeat the exercise, staying in the original character they had chosen.

EXAMPLE

The location might be a supermarket. The class brainstorms a mom, cashier, stock clerk, deli counter employee, janitor, manager, teens getting snacks, etc. When they break into pairs, Student A might take on a manager and Student B the fish counter person. They create an easy scene about how the area never smells clean enough and the manager tells the clerk to do more to keep the fish smell away. When the teams are reshuffled, the fish counter person might be paired up with a cashier and might be complaining about the manager, long work hours, etc.

PURPOSE OF ACTIVITY

Working to create characters based on the suggestion of a place means that you can create characters in scenes. Also, by discussing who might be at a specific location, students are expanding their ideas of what could take place in that scene. This is a way to generate a wider range of ideas and also increase the available world. This also teaches students to consider the point of view of each of the characters involved and play up those perspectives.

INTRODUCTORY MODIFICATIONS

N/A

ADVANCED MODIFICATIONS

Have students play characters they have never been or discuss a location that they have never been to before.

PITFALLS

Students often try to play the obvious character. Push them to explore with different characters in the environment. This will challenge them and help them grow as improvisors.

TIPS FOR COACHING

Ask the students to really try to understand what a person in their position would actually be concerned with and what their daily life is like. This exercise really turns on the points of view of a particular character, which helps lead to their behavior and dialogue.

PREREQUISITE SKILLS

Basic scene and character work

FUTURE SKILLS

Advanced character games (e.g., *Good/Bad Advice*; advanced scenes)

DEBRIEF

When discussing how things went, have students share a bit about the backstory of each of their characters – they will have learned more as their dialogues unfolded. Have them share what they liked or didn't like about their character and remind them that it is OK to play characters they don't like. Also, have students share why they were at the location so that they can give a little context to their character's motivation.

PENGUIN

OVERARCHING SKILL

Character development; personification

STRUCTURE OF ACTIVITY

Teacher writes suggestions on cards and hands them to students. Students then interact throughout the classroom.

DURATION OF ACTIVITY

10–15 minutes

EXPLANATION OF ACTIVITY

Teacher writes down on cards the names of animals based on half of the number of students (i.e., if there are eight students, the teacher writes a total of four animals, but writes each animal down twice). Each student is then given a card and they look at it without showing the other students. The object is to find the student with the matching card.

In the first round, the students cannot speak and must use movement alone to find their match. In the second round, they have to close their eyes and can only use the sound of the animal to find each other.

EXAMPLE

The teacher might write down elephant, duck, cat, and horse. For each animal, two students would be trying to represent their respective animal through movement alone as best as they can until they find each other. In the second round, and with different animals, they need to listen and use sound to represent their specific animal.

PURPOSE OF ACTIVITY

To show a character in multiple different ways and really understand the point of view of that character/animal. Important aspects of any character are how they think, what motivates them, and how they move in their environment. Using animals provides an easy way to practice showing those things.

INTRODUCTORY MODIFICATIONS

Start by having common animals and animals that are distinctly different.

ADVANCED MODIFICATIONS

To make this harder, have students be a human version of that animal that speaks English – have them converse with others and try to find the ones who are talking about the same things. For example, if you are a penguin and you are complaining to someone about how hot things are, and they respond that they love the heat and the desert, you are not a match and you need to move on to talk to others. If you find another person complaining about how cold it is, then you may have found your match – although equally your match may be talking about another aspect of their character, not just about the heat. This round can take a little longer so plan on it taking 15 minutes.

PITFALLS

Students don't always think they can fully show how that animal moves and interacts with the environment. Encourage them to really embody the animal they are portraying and really try to show all the details of that animal.

TIPS FOR COACHING

The more details they can provide about their animal, the easier it is to differentiate between similar ones. Ask the students how a cat moves versus how a dog moves – they are very different if you really consider it.

PREREQUISITE SKILLS

N/A

FUTURE SKILLS

Advanced scene work and games

DEBRIEF

During this debrief, try to relate what the students were doing to how they would be in a scene. Also discuss how they would show those characteristics as humans in a scene. If they played a turtle, how can they move and talk slower to make it a character that the audience can relate to. Also, this is an exercise in observing and listening to your stage partners so discuss how that went and how they can improve on that during scenes.

STATUS (W/ PLAYING CARDS)

OVERARCHING SKILL

Adjusting body postures, interactions, and conversation style based on character status

STRUCTURE OF ACTIVITY

Approximately eight to ten students are all on stage together. Each person gets a unique playing card, without looking at it. When instructed to do so, all students hold their card on their forehead facing out, so everyone else can see their card but they cannot.

DURATION OF ACTIVITY

5 minutes, plus 5 minutes to discuss

EXPLANATION OF ACTIVITY

Teacher prepares 13 unique playing cards and hands each of the eight to ten students one of the cards facing down (there will be several cards not handed out). On the teacher's signal, all the students hold their card up to their forehead, facing outward. They then have 3 minutes to interact with each other as if they are at a party. They are instructed to treat each other as you would treat a person at that status level (e.g., two is lowest on the totem pole). A good setup context is a large corporation, where students can imagine who a two is as opposed to an Ace, for example. Everyone is encouraged to interact with everyone else at some point during the 3 minutes, without telling other people what their card is, but treating them as they would a person in that position. At the end of the game, students line themselves up across the stage, in the position that they think they should be in, without discussing or directing each other. The teacher then reads off the cards and they discuss why they felt they were supposed to be in each spot.

EXAMPLE

N/A

PURPOSE OF ACTIVITY

To figure out your status in the game and how it relates to others while adjusting your interactions to ensure they are appropriate.

INTRODUCTORY MODIFICATIONS

You may need to start with more extreme examples (e.g., Kings and twos) instead of using cards more closely mixed together (e.g., 4, 5, 6). Also, you can start with just two players on stage to practice the power dynamics.

ADVANCED MODIFICATIONS

N/A

PITFALLS

Some students will take on a role that is too high or low status for their cards (i.e., they will degrade everyone else based on their belief that they are of a higher status than the first person they talked with). You'll need to help guide them to listen but also give clues without giving away the answer.

TIPS FOR COACHING

Feel free to coach students on physicality as well as verbal nuances of this game. If you are a two and talking to a Queen, that is going to be very different than if you are a two talking to a three. It is all very abstract, which is challenging, but encourage student's to just do their best to emphasize status in conversation. It could also help to give real-life examples (e.g., how you talk to your parent is different than how you talk to your Dr., which is different than how you talk to your sibling).

PREREQUISITE SKILLS

N/A

FUTURE SKILLS

Status can be built into scenes and is important for later games with partners and groups. This adds another layer to conversations and interaction games as well

DEBRIEF

Discuss what worked and what didn't. If students found the right order, talk about how they did it and what clues others gave that helped. If they didn't get the right order, talk about where they got confused and what they each could've done to help show their partner who they were. Also talk about who had it easiest and who had it hardest. Usually Aces and twos have it easier than middle cards, such as fives, sixes, and sevens. Discuss ways in which you can dial up the status without being mean/degrading.

SUPERHERO/SUPER VILLAIN

OVERARCHING SKILL

"Yes and . . ."; character creation

STRUCTURE OF ACTIVITY

Students start on stage, one at a time, followed by two-person scenes.

DURATION OF ACTIVITY

About 30 minutes+

EXPLANATION OF ACTIVITY

Students are given a minute or two on their own to plan a superhero or super villain character. Students then step on stage one at a time and explain the name of their new Superhero, where they came from, their origin story (i.e., how they got their powers), their weakness, and perhaps their mission in life. The class then asks them questions, which they answer, further developing their character. After everyone has done this, the teacher pairs up the students and they improvise a 1–2-minute scene with both their superheroes working either together or against each other in a given situation.

EXAMPLE

A student might say they are called Professor Ink. They are from London and they originally were bitten by a radioactive squid and filled with squid ink. Their superpower is that they can shoot ink out of their fingertips, blinding the bad guys and ruining their clothes. They can be hurt if they lose their hat and dry out. Their arch nemesis is named Dixon Ticonderoga, who is angry at always being called #2.

PURPOSE OF ACTIVITY

Students will have to come up with an entire storyline for their character and portray that character in different scenarios. The character creation aspect of this game is critical to decision making and relationships, which you will see when you set up the scenes later on.

INTRODUCTORY MODIFICATIONS

Start by keeping the storylines simple and to the point. Also, making the back-story short to begin with is helpful as well.

ADVANCED MODIFICATIONS

Expand on the relationship dynamics and build in the battles between heroes and villains.

PITFALLS

Students might build a complicated backstory then struggle to adjust their decision making in the scene aspect of this game. Also, scenes may just devolve into two people fighting, with no layering of plot or planning.

TIPS FOR COACHING

Make sure that the students have strong choices for their character and are not just basing them on classic characters. Also, remind students that if a character has a strong motivation for what they do, it will help drive dialogue.

PREREQUISITE SKILLS

Basic character and scene work

FUTURE SKILLS

More advanced character games (e.g., long-form)

DEBRIEF

Students will have a good time with this game. Talk about why they enjoyed their characters and what made them think of them in the first place. Ask if students have any ideas about the costume and other aspects of their hero/villian. For some students, the scene will be the hardest part. In essence, they are building a character and then putting that character into different interactions. Discuss what made that fun for them and how they felt their character may have developed across the various scenes.

THANKSGIVING DINNER

OVERARCHING SKILL

Character point of view; pantomime

STRUCTURE OF ACTIVITY

Students sit in a circle on stage recreating a Thanksgiving dinner.

DURATION OF ACTIVITY

10–15 minutes

EXPLANATION OF ACTIVITY

Students all sit in a circle on stage. One at a time they introduce themselves as a character that is made up or based on a real/fictional person. They then say what they are thankful for. The statement will help determine a bit more about their character. Once everyone has introduced themselves, the students act as if they are having an actual Thanksgiving dinner among friends, creating a scene with their characters.

EXAMPLE

One student might say in a snobby voice, "Hello, as you know, I'm Lady Davenport, and I'm thankful that all the less rich people are with me tonight, so that I can feel more grounded once a year." Another student might say, "Yo yo - I'm Rockin' Richie and I'm thankful that I'm gonna be busting out some fat beats for y'all tonight." During the ensuing scene, we might witness the clash between the two characters, since they are so different in personality, or a bond, since they both might have wealth in common.

PURPOSE OF ACTIVITY

By using a character's point of view, students can have in-depth conversations with friends they haven't seen in a while. They do that while pantomiming eating dinner and working to build interpersonal (and maybe conversational) skills. This game combines characters and pantomime, which are major parts of quality scenes.

INTRODUCTORY MODIFICATIONS

Have the students pick a character that everyone would know or have an idea about.

ADVANCED MODIFICATIONS

Allow students to make up entirely new characters.

PITFALLS

Students default to chaos in this scene. They might start by throwing bread and yelling over each other. Remind them that they should be having a realistic family-style dinner, which includes proper manners, like passing the bread, sharing with others, etc. Also remind them that their characters have interesting lives/perspectives and we want to hear about them.

TIPS FOR COACHING

Students need to yield the floor to each other when they start talking so there is no overlap. Also, look for areas where characters can create some level of conflict or resolution based on who they are, their value systems, etc.

PREREQUISITE SKILLS

Basic character ideas; pantomime

FUTURE SKILLS

Advanced scenes

DEBRIEF

It might be difficult to hear and check in with each student. Share as a group what events happened and what was worth highlighting. How have things gone since you saw your friend last year and what story lines unfolded? Also discuss with students the fact that they just created a scene – we could have easily let small groups be on stage and that would've been a great scene worth watching. They can bring back these ideas when they are doing scenes in the future and combine character and pantomime to create a unique reality.

EMOTION-BASED GAMES

Perhaps the category of games that is hardest to master is also the most important.

Emotion-based games are critical for good improvisation and building socially connected relationships. One of the entertaining aspects of building a scene is seeing two characters respond differently to the same situation. By showing this emotion, there is a human connection rather than just entertainment. Audiences are captivated by characters. But part of what makes characters so genuine is their emotional reaction. When audiences have the opportunity to empathize with a character, they instantly become connected and invested in the scene.

These types of games can be very therapeutic but also require an extra bit of bravery on stage. It takes courage to portray all the different emotions we think or experience on any given day. So much of our daily lives is about suppressing or minimizing emotions. These games require us to play them in their most extreme forms. The ultimate goal is for a student to stand on stage and actually feel the emotion their character would feel and show that in such a way that is believable and relatable.

The games outlined in this section are about showing emotion in several ways. The first is through body movements and postures – learning to adjust how we walk, move, and pantomime will bring situations to life. If someone is upset, they walk differently than someone who is happy. If you are late for an interview, you move differently than if you are on your way to a movie.

Secondly, we show emotions through speech and tone. Not just what is said, which is very important, but also how it is said. Tone portrays more about emotion than the spoken words. When combining the physical with the verbal, we get a glimpse into the inner feelings of another person. This is both challenging and terrifying, but is important for any student.

Adjusting how we move physically and how we communicate verbally changes the interaction with others on stage and brings an extra layer of depth to the scene. By learning how to communicate with intention, students learn to expand the characters in their repertoire and create more complex interactions.

Doing this takes confidence and a willingness to be vulnerable. Most students put up walls when it comes to these games. They present as monotonous characters and are unwilling to let their guard down and show all the emotional ranges in their repertoire. These games are designed to break down those walls, allow for students to experience different feelings, play with portraying them in novel ways, and enjoy the process of adjusting the aspects of each emotion for different characters.

EMOTIONAL MIRROR

OVERARCHING SKILL

Portraying emotions

STRUCTURE OF ACTIVITY

Class split on both sides of the stage, with two people on stage at a time.

DURATION OF ACTIVITY

10 minutes

EXPLANATION OF ACTIVITY

The class is divided in two and lined up on both sides of the stage. One person from each line steps onto the stage. Student A demonstrates an emotion with dialogue/movement/facial expression. Student B must then figure out what emotion is being presented and portray that emotion too. Together, they create a very short, 30-second scene involving that emotion. The object is to both portray and read emotions accurately. Once the group has gone through the line, switch the order so that the B group becomes the A group, so all students have the opportunity to give and receive the opening lines.

EXAMPLE

Student A might enter the stage, stare at the ground with hunched shoulders, and say, "My Little League team lost in the championship." Student B could pick up on the emotion of "disappointed" and say, "That's a bummer . . . I heard that my team was completely disbanded after this season." Student A might say, "Oh really? I had been hoping that we would play each other next year . . .," etc.

PURPOSE OF ACTIVITY

To practice showing emotions with body postures, movements, gestures, and words is very important, particularly when relating to others on and off stage. By showing those emotions in scenes, it helps build a story that the audience can relate to and assists students in showing how they are feeling without actually saying how they are feeling. Reading that body language is a huge skill for any actor.

INTRODUCTORY MODIFICATIONS

Assign the students the problem and/or the emotion.

ADVANCED MODIFICATIONS

Try to play this game using as few words as possible.

PITFALLS

Many students start by labeling how they are feeling in the first line of the scene (e.g., "I'm so mad"). Try to have them give clues with their bodies and read clues that are being shown by others on stage. As the teacher, you may need to coach both students to turn up or down the cues.

TIPS FOR COACHING

Be sure that Student B allows the first to completely portray their emotion before jumping to a conclusion. Also, make sure Student A is very clear in presenting what their emotion is. Students should use not just their voice but their whole body to present their emotion realistically.

PREREQUISITE SKILLS

Basic scene work

FUTURE SKILLS

Advanced emotion/scene games (e.g., *Sync About It, I Feel/You Feel*)

DEBRIEF

When checking in with students, discuss what made clue-giving easy or hard for them. Talk about how they were standing, what gestures gave clear clues, which movements across stage really gave a visual as to how they were feeling. Also discuss what was hard to show about the emotion they picked or were given. Extreme examples are easy to show (furious, elated, angry), but others require a bit more nuance (jealous, apathetic). Talk about how they can give clues with words and tone but also body postures and movements.

EMOTIONAL SENTENCE

OVERARCHING SKILL

Showing emotions; reading emotions

STRUCTURE OF ACTIVITY

Students walk onto the stage, one at a time, stand downstage center, and recite a line of dialogue.

DURATION OF ACTIVITY

30 seconds per student

EXPLANATION OF ACTIVITY

One at a time, students will walk to the front center of the stage. The class will have previously suggested a simple sentence. Each student has to say the same sentence but with a different emotion behind it. The class then needs to guess the emotion.

EXAMPLE

The sentence is, "We've run out of food already." One student might deliver the line very sadly, a different student might be frightened about it, and a third might find it amusing. They deliver the line and allow their body posture and vocal intonation to indicate what the emotion is. The audience keeps guessing until they get it right.

PURPOSE OF ACTIVITY

To show emotion by adjusting body posture and movements and changing vocal intonation. For the audience, they need to be able to read those cues and interpret what is being said by those body postures and gestures.

INTRODUCTORY MODIFICATIONS

You may need to assign very clear emotions to get started (e.g., joyous, sad, angry).

ADVANCED MODIFICATIONS

As students become better, work to show more subtle emotions and include more body gestures.

PITFALLS

Students may default to angry or happy because they are easy to portray. Challenge them to push themselves to the extremes of those OR to include more difficult emotions.

TIPS FOR COACHING

Tell the student to imagine why they are saying the particular line with the emotion, and to express themselves very strongly. Students might deliver the line too subtly for the class to guess the emotion, so encourage them to play it large and to use both their voice and body to express the emotion.

PREREQUISITE SKILLS

N/A

FUTURE SKILLS

Sync About It; *I Feel/You Feel*; other scenes that require showing a range of emotions

DEBRIEF

Talk about what students showed, not just what they said. The underlying purpose of this game is to not only listen to what is said, but recognize HOW it is said. Also, body postures can change the intent of the person on stage. They need to be aware of how their emotions are shown so they can adjust their delivery of the line as needed, but also be aware of what the audience may expect given that specific emotion.

I FEEL/YOU FEEL

OVERARCHING SKILL

Bringing emotions into scenes and showing them to peers

STRUCTURE OF ACTIVITY

Two students on stage together in a short scene.

DURATION OF ACTIVITY

2–3 minutes per group

EXPLANATION OF ACTIVITY

Two students start on stage and each is given a different emotion. They are given a single location and then play out a short scene in that location while feeling their emotion. The scene, and emotion played, can be about where they are, who they're with, or what their circumstances are.

EXAMPLE

One student is given "happy," the other "nervous." They are playing a scene at a football stadium. The happy student says that they are thrilled they finally got tickets, that their seats are great, their team is going to win, etc. Meanwhile, the nervous student mentions that the seats are too high in the air, their car might be broken into. They also might be slowly working up their courage to propose to the happy student but are worried the answer will be no.

PURPOSE OF ACTIVITY

To develop students' ability to read and show emotions in various ways. The audience wants to see how students portray emotions by what they say, how they say it, and how they interact with the environment. By giving them an emotion that drives all of their decisions, students can use that to shape their character.

INTRODUCTORY MODIFICATIONS

Have students be different emotions in normal locations.

ADVANCED MODIFICATIONS

Have students show the same emotion but in a location that would typically not be aligned with that emotion (e.g., both students are sad at Disneyland). Work on portraying the juxtaposition of those emotions with that location.

PITFALLS

Students may need help reading and showing emotions with their physicality on stage. They often switch emotions to match what the other person is showing as well.

TIPS FOR COACHING

The scene is not about the emotion itself but about the situation and *why* they are feeling the emotion. Be sure that students actually feel their emotion in a big enough way so that their scene partner and the audience can see it.

PREREQUISITE SKILLS

Basic emotion-based games

FUTURE SKILLS

More advanced scene work; more complicated emotional games

DEBRIEF

Focus your debrief on the emotions of the game and how students felt showing these to their stage partners. Was it easy to start an emotion? Was it hard to bring that emotion into each aspect of the character? If we didn't get to see it in the scene, what made that character feel that emotion? Having a backstory is a fun way to build a character and create strong scenes.

SILENT EMOTION

OVERARCHING SKILL

Showing emotions; pantomime

STRUCTURE OF ACTIVITY

One student at a time on stage.

DURATION OF ACTIVITY

About 30 seconds to 1 minute per student

EXPLANATION OF ACTIVITY

One at a time, students take the stage. They then act out, through pantomime only, an emotion that they have either come up with themselves or that the teacher has whispered to them. The class then needs to guess the emotion.

EXAMPLE

A student might step on stage and suddenly look around them with their eyes wide open. They may move pensively back and forth around the stage in a state of high alert. The class might raise their hands and guess "nervous" or "paranoid" until the student on stage agrees that the guess is correct.

PURPOSE OF ACTIVITY

Many students have difficulty showing and reading emotions. This is a way for them to practice doing both without being able to say how they are feeling. They are going to have to play up or down certain gestures and postures to really show their emotion. This gives the teacher insight into how students are reading emotions, and how students are going to show them in scenes.

INTRODUCTORY MODIFICATIONS

Teachers could give suggestions of the emotion or an environment for students to interact with.

ADVANCED MODIFICATIONS

Have students work this into a scene and try to show those emotions to get the scene started.

PITFALLS

Students will pick the easiest emotions to portray and shy away from more advanced ones. Encourage them to challenge themselves. Also, students will do one action instead of several (e.g., standing with arms crossed and involving no other actions) – work with them so they have multiple ways of demonstrating the emotion.

TIPS FOR COACHING

Students should attempt to think of a reason why they are feeling this particular emotion and act accordingly rather than just acting out the stereotype of the emotion. The more it is based on a real event, the more genuine the emotion will seem to them and the rest of the class.

PREREQUISITE SKILLS

N/A

FUTURE SKILLS

Emotion-based games and scenes (e.g., *Silent Tension*)

DEBRIEF

For some students, showing emotions will be very easy. They also might think they gave clear movements, when actually this may not be the case. Discuss what stood out as a group and what the students noticed. If there were incorrect guesses, reassure the class that this is OK. Discuss what mannerisms gave the impression of the incorrect guess and what the actor was trying to show with these mannerisms. It is always a good idea to discuss what the acting student's thought process was with the group.

SYNC ABOUT IT

OVERARCHING SKILL

Showing emotions; using pantomime

STRUCTURE OF ACTIVITY

Two lines of students on each side of the stage. One student enters the stage from one side, another enters from the other side and they create a scene.

DURATION OF ACTIVITY

10–15 minutes

EXPLANATION OF ACTIVITY

The class is divided into two lines, one on each side of the stage. A student from one of the lines enters the stage and starts to pantomime an activity while displaying an emotion. A second student from the other line enters and says, "I feel so _____," with the blank being the emotion that they sense the first student is displaying. They justify why they are feeling that emotion. The first student then continues the scene, agreeing with the emotional choice even if it wasn't an accurate guess. After a brief scene, the teacher clears the stage and two more students begin.

EXAMPLE

Student 1 might be stomping around the stage and washing dishes very angrily. Student 2 enters and says, "I feel so annoyed because there was a huge traffic jam getting here." Student 1 says, "Yeah, and the kids left all these dishes in the sink, after I told them a million times to put them in the dishwasher." They continue for a few more lines, both being "annoyed" at what's happening in the scene.

PURPOSE OF ACTIVITY

To show emotions to your stage partner by using gestures and body movements and letting them interpret those postures. This helps both students, in that Student 1 practices showing emotions and Student 2 practices reading and interpreting emotional cues.

INTRODUCTORY MODIFICATIONS

Teachers could start by giving students the emotions and a location to help focus the scenes.

ADVANCED MODIFICATIONS

You can expand this from emotions to an event that just happened (e.g., what happened right before the scene started). This adds a layer to the complexity of the scene and the story of the character.

PITFALLS

Students struggle with justifying how they are feeling and don't elaborate on it.

TIPS FOR COACHING

The initial student should have a reason as to why they are feeling their emotion, rather than just indicating the emotion. This will give their portrayal of the emotion more depth and make it easier to guess for the other student. Also, they need to be able to let go of their original choice if the guess by the second student isn't accurate.

PREREQUISITE SKILLS

Basic scene work and emotion games (e.g., *Silent Tension*)

FUTURE SKILLS

More advanced scene games that include justification (e.g., *Blind Line, Pan Left/ Pan Right*)

DEBRIEF

There are two challenging aspects to this game. The first is showing the emotion in a silent way and trying to get the other person to recognize how you are feeling. Discuss what body movements helped achieve this and how players showed their emotions. The second is the justification of that emotion. Discuss with players whether or not that was challenging and what strategies they used to overcome that. Remind them that anything their character says (provided it is in context with that reality) is the right answer.

YOU MAKE ME FEEL

OVERARCHING SKILL

Perspective taking; character development; scene work; emotion

STRUCTURE OF ACTIVITY

Two students on stage creating a scene.

DURATION OF ACTIVITY

2–3 minutes per group

EXPLANATION OF ACTIVITY

One student starts on stage and another then enters from off stage. The first student delivers a line to the entering student that labels them with some sort of quality (emotion, trait, etc.). A short scene then progresses from that point, incorporating what the first student had stated.

EXAMPLE

A student might be on stage pantomiming setting a table. The second student enters from off stage.

Student 1: "Terry, you're late again. You're always late to everything!"

Student 2: "Sorry Wendy, I missed the bus to get here. I got to the bus stop 5 minutes after the bus had already left."

Student 1: "Well, dinner is burned."

Student 2: "I lost track of time at work. I'd go out to buy us dinner, but I didn't send in my driver's license renewal in time."

Student 1: "This was just like our wedding day when you missed the ceremony."

Student 2: "Yeah, but my watch stopped overnight and I didn't realize it," etc.

PURPOSE OF ACTIVITY

This game covers many aspects that are important for good scene work. By being assigned a character trait, students have to respond to that and determine what else is true about that character. They also have to show the emotions, traits, actions, and movements of that character while adjusting their decision making to match.

INTRODUCTORY MODIFICATIONS

The teacher can give the character trait to each student while they are already on stage.

ADVANCED MODIFICATIONS

N/A

PITFALLS

Students often get stuck on the one example and don't expand that trait. Work on the concept of, "if this is true about my character, what else is true," to help them round out their character.

TIPS FOR COACHING

Students should be very quick to drop what they think the scene is about and "go with the flow." Very often a student enters and won't pick up on what has been assigned to them. The scene can grow from the conflict that is set up by the original line.

PREREQUISITE SKILLS

Basic scene work; character work; emotional portrayal

FUTURE SKILLS

Advanced scenes

DEBRIEF

This game has a lot of layers to it and can be complex. Ask students what worked in their scenes and how it felt to be assigned a character. Remind them that a character trait can be portrayed in several different ways. Ask students to expand on their characters and have them share a bit about what they considered or discovered about that character.

QUICK-THINKING/
DELIVERY GAMES

One of the more fun and entertaining categories of games and activities is focused on the participants having to answer quickly or come up with instant responses to suggestions. There are several takeaways from these activities, in addition to their entertainment value.

A very common issue is the concept of stage fright or shyness in front of a group. This is a universal fear that is best addressed in a number of ways. Within the context of this set of activities, the concept of "failure" not being an issue can lead a performer to begin to relax while on stage or in front of a group. Most of these activities have no "penalty" for an incorrect answer, and in fact, the answers that are not expected tend to be the more successful ones. Additionally, there are typically so many chances to step forward that a few "misses" here or there are vastly outweighed by the hits. A baseball player doesn't get upset after every strike, they just attempt to hit the ball the next time up.

There is also a common fear that when a person steps in front of a group of people their brain will suddenly freeze and they won't be able to speak or come up with an answer. By repeatedly demonstrating to a student that they are the same person with the same brain, regardless of whether they are facing the stage or facing the audience, students will begin to realize that the concept of stage fright is a mirage that we impose on ourselves. The activities in this section are easy whether one is on stage or not, and the lighthearted approach to them absolutely leads to a person feeling more comfortable in front of groups.

The second major theme when teaching/learning any of these activities is the development of solid presentation skills. A student will find that there is a vast difference in response from the audience if they speak clearly and project so that everyone in the room will hear them. Most students do not have a clear understanding of what they look like and sound like on stage, and their dialogue can become difficult to hear or comprehend. Many of these activities require a student to stand downstage facing front, delivering dialogue straight to the audience. This presents a very easy opportunity for the instructor to address issues of volume, stage wandering, enunciation, etc. When a performer plants their feet and speaks clearly, they project a more confident image, and the audience responds accordingly.

Public speaking is routinely considered the most common fear, and these activities confront it head on. Many of these games rely on a group of performers all being on stage together, and there is great comfort in that. Frequently, there is a breakthrough moment when the first performer kicks off a game, and then the others will follow. It is through repetition, positive reinforcement, refusal to define anything as a failure, and a sense of fun that the performers will be able to confront the idea that speaking in front of a group is a frightening thing and they will be able to relax and allow their personality to show on stage.

185

Creating puns; delivering jokes with good timing and emphasis

STRUCTURE OF ACTIVITY

Students tell a single joke with multiple punchlines.

DURATION OF ACTIVITY

10 minutes

EXPLANATION OF ACTIVITY

Students stand in a line against the back wall of the stage. The teacher picks a topic (e.g., profession, animal, object) and if a student comes up with a good joke/pun around that topic they step to the front center of the stage and deliver the following joke:

"185 (blanks) walk into a bar. The bartender says, 'Hey, we don't serve (blanks) here.' The (blanks) reply, (punchline).

This continues until the students cannot come up with a new joke, with a new topic then being chosen.

EXAMPLE

If the topic is doctors, a student might say, "185 doctors walk into a bar, the bartender says 'Hey, we don't serve doctors here,' the doctors reply 'that's OK, we just wanted a shot.'"

PURPOSE OF ACTIVITY

To build confidence and deliver an on-topic joke with good timing and with confidence. Also, to find creative puns and jokes from normal everyday items, become more comfortable with risk taking (i.e., standing in front of an audience and delivering jokes), and overcome failure (i.e., have the opportunity to tell another joke if one didn't go well).

INTRODUCTORY MODIFICATIONS

You could pick a topic and create a list of puns as a group; practice delivering lines with emphasis on the pun; create some stock puns and use them for various categories (doctor, nurse, hospital, veterinarian, etc.).

ADVANCED MODIFICATIONS

Pick more challenging topics that require a more advanced skill set for creating puns.

PITFALLS

Students have a hard time with understanding the topic of puns. You may need to do a few practice rounds so that they have a better understanding of the goal. Students will struggle with the delivery of the joke as well – work on the proper emphasis of the appropriate part of the punchline.

TIPS FOR COACHING

Students should use a loud and clear voice when delivering the joke. They should say the entire joke, even if there are four or five variations of the punchline from other students. Students should stay in their position until the punchline is delivered, rather than stepping back to the line while saying their joke.

PREREQUISITE SKILLS

Creating puns; feeling comfortable being alone on stage

FUTURE SKILLS

N/A

DEBRIEF

Discuss how using a confident voice made the jokes stronger. Also, the jokes that "fail" can be as funny as the jokes that work. The hardest part of the game is walking out to attempt the first joke, so it's all about the attempt rather than editing ideas to come up with the "correct" one.

ALPHABET

Group mindset; working together to achieve a goal

Students sit in a circle and provide answers to different categories.

10 minutes

Teacher and students sit in a circle. A category is chosen and the students, one at a time, have to say something that fits that category, going from A to Z. The object of each round is to make it to the letter "Z."

Category is animals.

Student 1: Antelope

Student 2: Beaver

Student 3: Cat

Student 4: Dog

etc.

Group mind is a big part of improv and working together to achieve a goal is critical for scene work and other games. This game builds on these foundational skills and on the camaraderie amongst the students. This also helps to create trust between players and motivates them to listen to each other more intently.

INTRODUCTORY MODIFICATIONS

Instead of trying to get all the way to Z, you could just go once around the circle.

ADVANCED MODIFICATIONS

It is possible to go from easier suggestions (names, animals, fruits, etc.) to harder ones (countries, cars, etc.). This can also be played as an elimination game.

PITFALLS

N/A

TIPS FOR COACHING

Change who starts each round so that students get a different letter each time. Tell students to quickly say the first thing that comes to their mind. If they are stuck, have them say the sound of the letter out loud to see what follows. This game isn't about speed, so support as needed. If a player gets stuck, open up to the group for suggestions.

PREREQUISITE SKILLS

N/A

FUTURE SKILLS

Storytelling games

DEBRIEF

Highlight that the purpose of this game is to get people working together and focused on what is coming, not about giving the "right" answer or the fastest answer. There isn't a win necessarily with this game, other than building team-work and trust amongst students.

BLIND FREEZE

OVERARCHING SKILL

Quick thinking; character development; story development

STRUCTURE OF ACTIVITY

Two students on stage with the rest of the class split on either side of the stage.

DURATION OF ACTIVITY

About 10 minutes

EXPLANATION OF ACTIVITY

Two students on stage randomly move about for a few seconds until the teacher yells "Freeze!" They freeze in position for a moment and then unfreeze and begin a scene that justifies why they were in that position. After a few beats (perhaps 15 seconds or so), the teacher again calls out "Freeze" and two new students come in and take the exact position that the original students are now in, beginning a new scene from there.

EXAMPLE

N/A

PURPOSE OF ACTIVITY

By using pantomime as a way to start scenes, students learn more about how to show their environment to the audience. This also teaches students to use the entirety of the space they are creating. This helps bring scenes to life and helps students use more of their abstract thinking skills.

INTRODUCTORY MODIFICATIONS

Play the activity with just four people, with a single person rotating in each time.

ADVANCED MODIFICATIONS

Individual "freezes" can be turned into complete scenes.

PITFALLS

Students tend to repeat common themes of "dancing" or "martial arts" or "monkeys." There is also the possibility of students becoming too physical or out of control during the game. It is critical to remind students to pay attention to each other and not allow anyone to be harmed.

TIPS FOR COACHING

Encourage students to take a beat before starting each scene to give themselves time to imagine what they are feeling when they are in that position, and what that triggers in their minds. They will have a much greater variety of scenes if they don't pre-plan but instead jump in and then sense what it feels like.

PREREQUISITE SKILLS

N/A

FUTURE SKILLS

Scene work; mime games

DEBRIEF

This game can be challenging when students are trying to start a scene from just a body posture. Discuss what was easier – standing and talking or moving around their space. Also, it is a good time to discuss pantomime and share what the audience noticed or what stood out. Was there some pantomiming that was really impressive? Highlight how it was easier to start a scene by just getting into the movements.

CATEGORIES

OVERARCHING SKILL

Giving on-topic details and thinking quickly while listening to others

STRUCTURE OF ACTIVITY

Approximately six to eight students standing across the stage facing the audience, providing quick answers to subjects supplied by the audience.

DURATION OF ACTIVITY

10 minutes

EXPLANATION OF ACTIVITY

Students stand shoulder to shoulder facing the audience. The teacher gets a general category (i.e., "desserts") from the audience. When pointed to, students need to say one thing that fits the category. The teacher kneels or stands in front of students and points to them randomly.

EXAMPLE

With everyone standing on stage, the suggestion might be "colors." You point to students, one at a time, and they say a color (red, yellow, green, blue, orange, etc.). Once they repeat or get stuck, move onto a new category.

PURPOSE OF ACTIVITY

To build confidence, practice listening to others on stage, practice stage presence, develop quick thinking skills, encourage students to say something and not freeze when put on the spot.

INTRODUCTORY MODIFICATIONS

Instead of pointing to people, you could go in a line so there is some predictability and students can plan their answers. Also, you could allow for more time or repeats to help students get started.

ADVANCED MODIFICATIONS

For advanced groups, each student gets two "strikes" before they are out. When a student repeats an answer or says something that doesn't fit the category, they have to raise one hand, indicating a strike. If they get two strikes, they sit down in the audience and the game continues until there is one "winner."

PITFALLS

Some students will repeat what was just said. Often when students don't have an answer they will freeze or yell out something unrelated.

TIPS FOR COACHING

Start each round slowly and pick up the pace as you continue. Tell students to try to brainstorm a list in their head, but also remind them to listen closely so they don't repeat a previous answer. Make sure the suggestions are not so esoteric that students will give up immediately or simply not know anything that fits the category.

PREREQUISITE SKILLS

N/A

FUTURE SKILLS

The skills from this can be used in scene work later or in character development (having confidence, saying something, embracing the mistake, etc.).

DEBRIEF

This game is about quick thinking and confidence on stage. Don't get too worried about what the categories were or how long the game went on for. Instead, focus on the underlying skills, like confidence and stage presence, that the game builds on.

EXPERT

OVERARCHING SKILL

Remaining on topic to improve socially appropriate conversations

STRUCTURE OF ACTIVITY

One student on stage with the rest sitting in the audience, raising their hands and asking questions.

DURATION OF ACTIVITY

10–15 minutes

EXPLANATION OF ACTIVITY

One person is given a specific topic and answers questions about that topic as quickly as possible with related answers. Students should not worry about giving accurate answers or logical answers but rather quick answers that are within the world of possibilities.

EXAMPLE

A student is given the topic of food. Q&A:

"What food is eaten the most around the world?"

"Spaghetti."

"What is the best restaurant in San Diego?"

"Pizza Hut."

"If I want to lose weight, what food should I eat?"

"Only breakfast foods."

"What foods are bad for the environment?"

"Broccoli."

"What is the healthiest food?"

"Tacos."

PURPOSE OF ACTIVITY

To build confidence, encourage rapid responses and saying the first appropriate thing that comes to mind, gain an understanding of the importance of timing of jokes (so adding to joke-telling ability), and work on "Yes, and . . ." as a concept.

INTRODUCTORY MODIFICATIONS

Use topics that are familiar to the student and mix in questions that the student might know the answer to. This game can also be done in partners so they can take turns.

ADVANCED MODIFICATIONS

Use more abstract ideas and concepts (e.g., religion, scientific thoughts, time periods in history, etc.).

PITFALLS

Students will fall into "I don't know" – encourage them to come out of that. They may also give repetitive, off-topic, or random answers to avoid having to think of a proper answer. Students also like to sink into the back of the stage and speak to the floor as they become less confident.

TIPS FOR COACHING

Push for more details and specifics if answers are vague. Throw in your own questions to challenge students or give them an easy question when you feel the timing is right. Praise good, detailed, on-topic answers that are given with confidence.

PREREQUISITE SKILLS

N/A

FUTURE SKILLS

More advanced "Yes, and . . ." games (e.g., *Story*); other Q&A games (e.g., *Good/Bad Advice*, *Dr. Know-It-All*); justification games (e.g., *Blind Line*, *Pan Left/Pan Right*, *Blind Freeze*)

DEBRIEF

Talk about how it felt to be alone on stage and make sure to give lots of praise for that – it is a great skill and also very challenging for students. Try to push them to think more about giving details in their answers and highlight a few answers that stood out. This will help them give an on-topic and detailed answer with confidence, which will be funnier than a vague answer. Also, consider that their answer could be a denial rather than a "yes, and . . ." to the question. The answer should elaborate on the question (e.g., "no" vs. "no because of _____").

HEY WAITER

OVERARCHING SKILL

Puns; joke delivery

STRUCTURE OF ACTIVITY

Students stand shoulder to shoulder against the back wall of the stage. One at a time, students randomly step forward and deliver a pun.

DURATION OF ACTIVITY

10 minutes

EXPLANATION OF ACTIVITY

The teacher picks a suggestion of an object or occupation and then delivers the line, "Hey waiter, there's a (suggestion) in my soup." If a student has an idea, they then step forward and deliver a pun to describe what the solution might be. After a few puns are delivered, the teacher picks a new suggestion. This is typically played with five or six different suggestions per round.

EXAMPLE

Suggestion is: pencil.

Teacher: "Hey Waiter, there's a pencil in my soup."

Student 1: "Let me get write on that."

Teacher: "Hey Waiter, there's a pencil in my soup."

Student 2: "This problem is number 2 for me."

Teacher: "Hey Waiter, there's a pencil in my soup."

Student 3: "I get the point."

PURPOSE OF ACTIVITY

To deliver a pun-based joke with confidence.

INTRODUCTORY MODIFICATIONS

You may need to start by making a list of pun options and then helping them work out the delivery.

ADVANCED MODIFICATIONS

N/A

PITFALLS

Students struggle with the concept of puns and will instead just offer to fix the soup. Work with students to ensure some type of joke is included.

TIPS FOR COACHING

Students should deliver the line with confidence. When thinking of a pun, have them free associate all words that are connected with the suggestion to see if any with two different meanings might work as the pun.

PREREQUISITE SKILLS

N/A

FUTURE SKILLS

Other pun-based games (e.g., *185*)

DEBRIEF

When debriefing with students, focus on the delivery of the joke. The more confidence they portray on stage, the funnier the joke will be. They will struggle with delivering the lines with a punch, but that will come over time. Discuss which items were easier in terms of coming up with associated puns and which ones were harder. Have them practice making puns outside of class as well.

I DECLARE/PREDICT

OVERARCHING SKILL

Presenting on stage with confidence; creating an alternate reality

STRUCTURE OF ACTIVITY

One student on stage at a time.

DURATION OF ACTIVITY

10 minutes

EXPLANATION OF ACTIVITY

Teacher picks an object suggested by the class. One at a time, students step on stage and make a prediction about that object. They then field questions from the class about their prediction. After 30 seconds to 1 minute, another student makes a different prediction about the same object.

EXAMPLE

The subject is cell phones.

Student 1: "I predict that by 2025 cell phones will be tiny and implanted into our fingertips." (Students then ask two to three questions about this.)

Student 2: "I predict that in the next 10 years, cell phones will achieve consciousness and start giving us orders."

(Students ask questions.)

Student 3: "I predict that the next administration will ban the use of cell phones and we'll go back to rotary dial," etc.

PURPOSE OF ACTIVITY

This game has several skills going on at the same time. First, it involves getting up on stage in front of an audience and making a statement with confidence, which can be hard to do. Second, it is about exploring various aspects of a topic so as not to repeat a previous student's response. This requires the student to think of all the ways in which you can key in on a topic, which can lead to a wider variety of scenes with more varied realities.

INTRODUCTORY MODIFICATIONS

N/A

ADVANCED MODIFICATIONS

N/A

PITFALLS

Students will often repeat what others have said or use that as a similar talking point for their declaration. Work to have them create their own and not get too impacted by previous statements.

TIPS FOR COACHING

Students should speak with confidence, as if they have studied the subject and they are experts at it. Encourage them to think about what the natural progression of this particular object could be.

PREREQUISITE SKILLS

N/A

FUTURE SKILLS

Using this as a scene generator would be a good exercise for more advanced students

DEBRIEF

This game is a bit silly and does not require too much skill. Discuss with students why we do this game and what else we are working on when we play games like this. Also, encourage them to share what they noticed as audience members (confidence, voice projection, posture on stage, etc.)

QUICK ANSWER

OVERARCHING SKILL

Quick thinking; "yes, and . . ."

STRUCTURE OF ACTIVITY

One student on stage answering rapid fire questions from the audience.

DURATION OF ACTIVITY

1–2 minutes per student

EXPLANATION OF ACTIVITY

A student stands on stage and the class asks them questions on anything – their life, general knowledge, etc., provided their questions are based on real life. The student must answer the questions as quickly as possible with their best possible answer. Answers don't have to be "correct," they just have to be fast.

EXAMPLE

Questions/answers could be:

"What's your favorite food?"

"Pizza"

"What do you want to do for a living?"

"Fireman"

"What's the biggest bird?"

"Condor"

"Is there life on Mars?"

"Yes, mostly octopus"

"How tall are you?"

"5'10"

PURPOSE OF ACTIVITY

To think quickly. This is a skill that needs practice, similar to pantomime and other skills. The purpose here is simply to practice giving a fast answer that is based on the reality of the question – actually giving an answer is key.

INTRODUCTORY MODIFICATIONS

You could pick a specific topic if that helps some people (this is easier for both those asking and answering questions).

ADVANCED MODIFICATIONS

Allow for increased flexibility and slightly extend the limitations of our common reality.

PITFALLS

Many students get stuck thinking or simply say, "I don't know." In order to move onto the next question, students must give an answer regardless of how accurate it is. The purpose of this game is not to be accurate but to be as fast as possible while giving a realistic answer.

TIPS FOR COACHING

Students should not be concerned with getting the correct answer (or asking the "correct" question). They should just keep it as quick as possible and answer with confidence and realistically.

PREREQUISITE SKILLS

Standing in front of audience; basic "yes, and . . ."

FUTURE SKILLS

Other reality-changing games (e.g., *Expert, Story*)

DEBRIEF

For some students answering questions will be the easier task compared to asking questions. Discuss which was easier and how students felt being on stage by themselves. If you gave a specific topic, talk about how that made it easier for them to ask or answer the questions. Discuss how it felt to give quick answers vs. giving thoughtful and accurate answers. Also, discuss how it seems more realistic when an answer is given with confidence and includes a detail. The yes/no answer is OK every now and then, but the better answer is "yes because flying south is harder in summer."

TRY THAT ON FOR SIZE

OVERARCHING SKILL

Pantomime

STRUCTURE OF ACTIVITY

Two students on stage at the same time.

DURATION OF ACTIVITY

About 1 minute per pair

EXPLANATION OF ACTIVITY

Two students stand on stage a few feet apart. The teacher suggests an activity and one starts pantomiming the activity. The other student matches the same movement, which they do repeatedly (e.g., swinging a golf club over and over). The first student says the activity, followed by the words, "Try that on for size." The second student then says a different activity, but one that would use the exact same movement, followed by, "Try that on for size," and it goes back and forth between the two, always changing the content of what they are saying while continuing to act out the same activity.

Attempt for at least three responses per student. The game should continue until one person cannot come up with a response, or the teacher can stop it after enough responses.

EXAMPLE

If the suggestion is golf, it might go:

Student 1: "I'm playing golf, try that on for size."

Student 2: "I'm cutting weeds with a weed wacker, try that on for size."

Student 1: "I'm the pendulum of a clock, try that on for size."

Student 2: "I'm ringing a large bell, try that on for size."

Student 1: "I'm using a metal detector, try that on for size," etc.

PURPOSE OF ACTIVITY

This game will help students be more creative with their pantomime and consider other ways they can use their bodies in space. Without the prop, actions can take on various meanings depending on how you justify them or explain them.

INTRODUCTORY MODIFICATIONS

Start with very predictable actions from well-known situations. Also, everyone can work collaboratively to come up with ideas if needed to help students initially understand the concept.

ADVANCED MODIFICATIONS

N/A

PITFALLS

Students get stuck on one particular aspect of their gesture. If the motion is kicking, they will change what they are kicking but not the action itself (e.g., kicking a ball, kicking a cat, kicking a shoe, kicking the fence). Work to have them expand the action as well. Also, remind students to keep doing the action – this will help them be creative.

TIPS FOR COACHING

If a student is stuck, just have them continue doing the motion for a bit and ask them what else it feels like or might look like from the outside. Typically, students will quit the game as soon as they start to run out of ideas, but if they are pushed to stay in, they usually can break through this and come up with more ideas. Finally, students struggle with abstract concepts such as pantomime, so expect this game to be very challenging.

PREREQUISITE SKILLS

Basic pantomime work

FUTURE SKILLS

Advanced scenes and pantomime games

DEBRIEF

Pantomime is very challenging for our students. Games like this will be very hard and require extra concentration on their part. Praise them for their effort and discuss with them things they noticed. What worked for each student? What gestures were easier or harder for this game? Also, discuss how we can use gestures to bring our scenes to life and ways we can be using pantomime in other games.

WHAT ARE YOU DOING?

OVERARCHING SKILL

Free association; stage presence

STRUCTURE OF ACTIVITY

Students line up on both sides of stage (off stage). Two students at a time stand on stage facing each other.

DURATION OF ACTIVITY

About 1 minute per pair

EXPLANATION OF ACTIVITY

Two students stand on stage facing each other, but cheating out to the audience. Cheating out means facing at a 45-degree angle, so on stage it looks like you are facing each other but you are also facing some of the audience. A suggestion is given (typically some sort of activity) and Student 1 begins miming this activity. Student 2 then says, "What are you doing!?" (This is delivered in a demanding tone of voice.) Student 1 stops, turns to Student 2 and replies with any activity OTHER than what they are miming, but still related to the suggestion.

Student 2 then mimes whatever Student 1 says and the process repeats in reverse. When actually doing the mime activity, students also add a verbal element to it as well, whether it's dialogue, sound effects, etc.

The game can also be played using two letters instead of a suggestion to set up the answers.

EXAMPLE

Suggestion is baseball. *Student 1 mimes swinging a bat.*

Student 2: "What are you doing!?"

Student 1: "Stealing home."

Student 2 mimes picking up home plate as if they're stealing it.

Student 1: "What are you doing?"

Student 2: "Using my bat as a toothpick."

Student 1 mimes holding a large bat in his teeth and complaining about the corn on the cob they ate earlier.

If played with letters, it might look like this:

Letters are S and C.

Student 1 starts miming jumping a rope.

Student 2: "What are you doing!?"

Student 1: "Stuffing a Cat."

Student 2 says, "Come here mittens" and mimes stuffing cotton into a cat.

Student 1: "What are you doing?"

Student 2: "Slapping a crab."

Student 1 mimes grabbing a crab and then slapping it, getting pinched by a claw and yelping, etc.

PURPOSE OF ACTIVITY

The purpose of this game is to create associations and strengthen A to B thinking (e.g., if I'm in this reality, what else is true). This game also helps strengthen students' ability to come up with quick one-line jokes and deliver them with confidence on stage in front of an audience.

INTRODUCTORY MODIFICATIONS

Go very slow and possibly add a pause between each ask to help students get into the flow.

ADVANCED MODIFICATIONS

N/A (this game is hard enough; we don't need to make it harder)

PITFALLS

Students often freeze on stage and get stuck thinking about what they actually do with the item suggested or at the place suggested. Additionally, students don't add in extra details, which can mean the suggestions lack depth.

TIPS FOR COACHING

The command should be barked at each other. Also, when using letters, have the students actually sound out the letter when they get stuck rather than just trying to think of the right word. A word will usually follow if they begin to actually pronounce the letter.

This is a high energy game – the bigger the energy, the more likely answers will flow.

PREREQUISITE SKILLS

Basic pantomime skills

FUTURE SKILLS

Advanced pantomime and free association games (e.g., *Categories*)

DEBRIEF

There are a lot of moving pieces to this game. Start by checking in to make sure everyone understands the structure of the game. Students will have a hard time with the mechanics of the game, which will slow them down, but remind them that this is OK to start – as they get settled the ideas will start flowing more quickly. Talk with students about how they came up with their ideas and what tricks they tried that seemed to help. Some students will struggle with the purpose of this game as many of them are very goal oriented and so they won't understand why this game is played. Have a conversation about how this game can help in other scenes and pantomime games and that doing things for FUN is also valuable.

WORLD'S WORST

OVERARCHING SKILL

Confident delivery; stage presence

STRUCTURE OF ACTIVITY

Students stand in a line across the back of the stage. One student steps to the front of the group at random times.

DURATION OF ACTIVITY

About 10 minutes

EXPLANATION OF ACTIVITY

Students line up across the back of the stage, facing the audience. The teacher picks a suggestion (e.g., occupation, social event, professional situation, product) and if any student has an idea, they can step forward and deliver the world's worst line that a person in that situation can deliver. Several students can go, one at a time, per suggestion before changing suggestions.

EXAMPLE

Suggestion is: World's Worst thing for a doctor to say.

Student 1 steps forward: "I think hand washing is overrated."

Student 2 steps forward: "Hmmm . . . I've never actually done this before."

Student 3 steps forward: "I don't have a medical degree, but I stayed at a Holiday Inn Express last night."

Student 4 steps forward and sneezes on the invisible patient.

Student 5 steps forward: "I think surgical masks are a violation of my civil rights," etc.

PURPOSE OF ACTIVITY

To deliver on-topic punchlines that include detail and are delivered with confidence – that is the formula for funny. Having students practice this skill in this format is a fun way to practice combining all of those elements and practice being in front of an audience.

INTRODUCTORY MODIFICATIONS

Keep suggestions to familiar categories.

ADVANCED MODIFICATIONS

N/A

PITFALLS

Students get stuck saying any aspect of whatever the category is or they give a good scenario that relates to the suggestion. Work on finding a bad thing that isn't necessarily the worst thing (the worst thing can get offensive to some). Allow students to find the rhythm in their delivery, as it will be beneficial in other games/scenes.

TIPS FOR COACHING

Short answers are typically better delivered than long and involved answers. Also, make sure that students keep the answers appropriate for the classroom.

PREREQUISITE SKILLS

N/A

FUTURE SKILLS

Longer delivery on stage (e.g., monologues, scene games that start with one person)

DEBRIEF

Talk with students about how they came up with their ideas, what worked, what didn't, and how they felt on stage. Remind students that stage confidence is so important and how they present is often more important than what they actually say. Their confidence and delivery can make or break their joke.

I always knew my kiddo marched to the beat of his own drum, but what we were missing was other drummers he could jam with; about 3 years ago, our son found his crew!

While we had tried various activities, ones for typical kids, ones for kids with various disabilities, we never found a good fit for our child.

My son is a happy, hilarious, autistic teen. He loves comedy, dancing, being silly, and most of all, making people laugh. When his therapist told us about an improv crew for teens on the spectrum, we could not sign up fast enough, and soon we began our weekly haul, in traffic, to meet with his Connections crew.

I knew that he would love it before we even started, what I did not understand was how it would shape our kid's life and bring him opportunities and experiences that we could previously have only dreamed of.

In the past 3 years, we have seen the ripple effects of the improv program in all aspects of our son's life.

Not only does he meet weekly with his crew to practice improv, those skills have made him more social, confident, and outgoing at school, home, and in our neighborhood. He no longer takes medication, and he has performed publicly with his crew for live audiences and made our parental hearts swell with joy with each new hurdle he leaps over.

The biggest and best surprise has been the social aspect. My child now regularly attends birthday parties, backyard hangouts, and texts and calls with his core group of improv friends. This is an absolute gift, to see him doing typical teenage activities – it's all that any of us want for our kids.

Jessica, Parent of 19-year-old teen

CHAPTER 4

SAMPLE CURRICULUM

Outlined in this section is a sample curriculum for the first six weeks of class. During this time, you should be focusing on teaching the warmup games, the class structure, and giving everyone a small taste of what is coming over the next few weeks – you are teaching the foundation for future classes.

Don't worry too much about diving into each game. Instead, look to build trust and communication amongst the group. Remember, you are asking a lot of each student. Have them take small steps towards understanding improv philosophy and they will be more successful.

There are some key things to notice about this first six-week sample. All of the categories of games are introduced during this time period. Generally, you should be building each category of game into your monthly lesson planning. During this initial six-week period, this is done partially to enable the teacher to assess student skills and strengths, but also to show students that a variety of games will be introduced. Students should be reminded that if they are strong in one category, they may struggle in another – and that is OK. This dynamic will set up opportunities for students to both be a model and have a model. Also, note that there is NOT an even distribution of games among the categories. This is not important, as you will have different focuses later on as you dive deeper into various skills.

As you expand beyond this initial six-week period, keep in mind the diversity of games and game categories. You should be hitting each game category multiple times per month. This will help develop new skills, improve strengths, and prevent boredom. It is also good to revisit games as skills progress and develop, but

DOI: 10.4324/9781003207627-4

ensure you find the balance between building on what they learned previously and the game becoming redundant.

If you are deciding to focus on a specific category of games for a month, it works best to practice that type of game each week. For example, if pantomime is a category that really needs work, practice some type of pantomime game each week while also hitting the various other categories as well. This will improve the skill but also avoid frustration for harder categories.

This sample six weeks is a loose guide for those starting a new class. Changing the order of games is fine, but the idea of starting with the easiest games and concepts will help create a few foundational skills. Dive in and have fun while being systematic about game choice and skill development. Most of the games for this initial six-week period do not have prerequisite skills, making them good places to start. This will help students experience some success while building relationships with others.

SAMPLE SCHEDULE: WEEK 1

GAME	EXPLANATION	FORMAT & SETUP	WHY?
Opening	Start with two deep breaths to help the class get centered and focused. I always say, "Let's take two deep breaths . . . one . . . and one more . . . that is our cue to leave everything out there, out there, and just be here." We then share the smallest positive thing that happened since you saw them last. SMALLEST thing, not a huge thing. Since it is their first week, have them say their name as well. Discuss a few rules for them to follow and try to get them to come up with their own rules about being respectful, keeping things PG, keeping volume appropriate, etc.	Whole group; standing in a circle on stage

5–10 minutes | Taking a moment to practice some positivity will help set the tone for class each week. This is also a great way to check in with each student and relax any tension they may have from their day. Additionally, this helps students practice communicating with each other in a safe space. |
| Name Game | Have them say their name and an action that goes with it. Then everyone says hi to that person and does the action. Example: "I'm Richie and I like to jump" (said while jumping), then everyone says, "Hi Richie" (while they jump). Go quickly here, there is no need to linger. | Whole group; standing in a circle on stage

5–10 minutes | This game is a way to help students learn each other's names. This is also a fun and silly introduction to the class and an easy way to welcome new students. This also exposes students to pantomime, which will be very challenging for them later. |

GAME	EXPLANATION	FORMAT & SETUP	WHY?
Zip Zap Zop	Students take turns pointing to each other and saying Zip, Zap, Zop. You start by pointing to someone and saying Zip, they then point to someone else and say Zap, they then point to a different person and say Zop. That repeats until someone makes a mistake, at which point everyone leans into the middle of the circle and says "Aah–Ooh–Gah!"	Whole group; standing in a circle on stage 5–10 minutes	Typically done first in a warmup. It is a chance for everyone to speak in a unified voice, to move quickly without overthinking, and to deal with failure at a very simple activity without repercussion.

GAME	EXPLANATION	FORMAT & SETUP	WHY?
Yes, and . . . Interview	Start by explaining that the point of this game is to get people to expand on whatever their partner says. The first rule of improv is "Yes, and . . . ", so that is what will be practiced here. Give students different topics that they will then make statements about. Their job is to answer your questions about their specified topic with, "yes, and . . . ", then expand on what you said. Start by introducing them to the audience and picking the topic they are experts in (e.g., animals, foods, vehicles, countries, sports, etc.). Ensure you make it something they are NOT really an expert in. You might start like, "ladies and gentlemen, we have here the world's leading expert on koalas. I heard you studied the koalas for over ten years." Then see where the conversation goes and expand on whatever they give to you. Spend a little bit of time with each person on stage in front of everyone, if possible. YOU ARE THE INTERVIEWER.	You on stage with one person at a time. Each interview should be 1–2 minutes Total game time: 10–20 minutes for a class size of 10	This activity is all about expanding on the conversation in a way that is still relatively on topic. In the shoelace example given in the individual game plan, all those statements are possible given that person is an expert. Those occurrences are all a possibility for that person but are also all on topic. It is important to be able to have flexibility in a conversation but also be a contributor so the other person isn't doing all the talking (or listening). This game is about finding that balance and having a back-and-forth conversation.

GAME	EXPLANATION	FORMAT & SETUP	WHY?
	Story is another way to expand on practice of "Yes, and . . ." skills. Start by explaining that you are going to write a story, one word at a time. It is best to have everyone start in a circle for this and just go around the group. Usually the first story will get crazy and go in all sorts of weird places. That is OK, let that happen. After the first round, give some feedback about staying on topic and maintaining the reality of the story (staying in the correct realm). Then try it again with a new starting word and a new title. Hopefully, it should have gone a bit better this time — if so, make sure you encourage your students.	Sitting in a circle 15–20 minutes	Students will have to work on creating a unique universe by combining listening skills, collective mind, and "yes, and . . ." skills. This means that if they have an idea, they may be able to work it in, but they may also be forced to abandon the idea.
Story	After that, adapt the game so one sentence is added at a time and then do a round with a new title. Talk with the group about which was easier for them and which made the most sense. The goal is to get them to develop their group mind thinking while building on a common story.		Students will have to learn to work together and share ownership of the story.

GAME	EXPLANATION	FORMAT & SETUP	WHY?
Good/Bad Advice	This is a quick, fun game to end class. You are on stage as a moderator or acting as host for a game show where the audience asks questions seeking advice. These questions can be about anything (e.g., How do I get out of doing homework? What should I do to get an allowance? My brother is mean, what trick can I play on him?) The player in the first chair gives good advice that people would like to hear, while the player in the second chair gives bad advice that would not be good to follow. Answer two to three questions then switch to the next group of players.	Teacher acting as host fielding questions from audience; two people on stage 10–15 minutes	To answer questions on topic and with details using a character's perspective, and strengthening students' ability to be on stage in front of an audience for longer time periods.

GAME	EXPLANATION	FORMAT & SETUP	WHY?
Closing	Take turns with students sharing something that was really fun or something that they learned. I usually go last and try to give them praise for efforts and highlight a few key things that happened this week. It is good to share that you are happy that they are all there and willing to be open to trying new things. Some of them might have felt good about class and others maybe not, but the first session is always interesting. End with all hands in the middle doing an "Aah-Ooh-Gah!"	Whole group; standing in a circle on stage 5 minutes	Getting them to debrief about the positive experience will keep them positive moving forward and will help them find success as improvisors.

SAMPLE SCHEDULE: WEEK 2

GAME	EXPLANATION	FORMAT & SETUP	WHY?
Opening	Start with two deep breaths to help the class get centered and focused. I always say, "Let's take two deep breaths . . . one . . . and one more . . . that is our cue to leave everything out there, out there, and just be here." We then share the smallest positive thing that happened since you saw them last. SMALLEST thing, not a huge thing.	Whole group; standing in a circle on stage

5–10 minutes | Taking a moment to practice some positivity will help set the tone for class each week. This is also a great way to check in with each student and relax any potential tension they may have from their day. Additionally, this helps students practice communicating with each other in a safe space. |
| Name Game | Have them say their name and an action that goes with it. Then everyone says hi to that person and does the action. Example: "I'm Richie and I like to jump" (said while jumping), then everyone says, "Hi Richie" (while they jump). Go quickly here, there is no need to linger. | Whole group; standing in a circle on stage

5–10 minutes | This game is a way to help students learn each other's names. This is also a fun and silly introduction to the class and an easy way to welcome new students. This also exposes students to pantomime, which will be very challenging for them later. |

GAME	EXPLANATION	FORMAT & SETUP	WHY?
Go	The basic goal of the game is to get students moving and laughing. One person comes to the middle of the circle, calls someone's name, and then takes their spot in the circle. That person comes to the middle and then calls someone else's name. This practices names and also provides a fun way to move around the space and get warmed up.	Whole group; standing in a circle 5–10 minutes	This game is great at teaching students to remember each other's names while moving around the stage and the circle. This is also good for practicing making mistakes and doing so in a fun and light way. It is also a good mechanism for making clear choices and communicating clearly to others on stage.
Zip Zap Zop	Students take turns pointing to each other and saying Zip, Zap, Zop. You start by pointing to someone and saying Zip, they then point to someone else and say Zap, they then point to a different person and say Zop. That repeats until someone makes a mistake, at which point everyone leans into the middle of the circle and says "Aah-Ooh-Gah!"	Whole group; standing in a circle on stage 5–10 minutes	Typically done first in a warmup. It is a chance for everyone to speak in a unified voice, to move quickly without overthinking, and to deal with failure at a very simple activity without repercussion.

GAME	EXPLANATION	FORMAT & SETUP	WHY?
Animal Clue	One person at a time introduces themselves but doesn't say what kind of animal they are. They are trying to give clues and see if others can guess. They can stand up straight and speak in English, but they are trying to share some information about their chosen animal and maybe walk and talk like that animal. For example, "Hi, I'm Tony. I eat flies and I live in a web. Lots of people like me at Halloween and I have eight legs." The class can ask questions if they are unsure what animal is being represented, and then the whole class can act out being that animal (only do this if they are settled enough to handle it).	One person on stage with audience guessing; then the whole group pretends to be the animal 10–15 minutes	Being on stage in front of people can be challenging. The purpose of this game is to help students feel comfortable being on stage while they practice giving the audience clues that are not too obvious. They can also work on building puns into their monologue and answering questions on the spot.

Story is another way to expand on practice of "Yes, and . . ." skills. Start by explaining that you are going to write a story, one word at a time. It is best to have everyone start in a circle for this and just go around the group. Usually the first story will get crazy and go in all sorts of weird places. That is OK, let that happen. After the first round, give some feedback about staying on topic and maintaining the reality of the story (staying in the correct realm). Then try it again with a new starting word and a new title. Hopefully, it should have gone a bit better this time – if so, make sure you encourage your students. After that, adapt the game so one sentence is added at a time and then do a round with a new title. Talk with the group about which was easier for them and which made the most sense. The goal is to get them to develop their group mind thinking while building on a common story.

Story

Sitting in a circle

15–20 minutes

Students will have to work on creating a unique universe by combining listening skills, collective mind, and "yes, and . . ." skills. This means that if they have an idea, they may be able to work it in, but they may also be forced to abandon the idea. Students will have to learn to work together and share ownership of the story.

GAME	EXPLANATION	FORMAT & SETUP	WHY?
Yes, and . . . Interview	Start by explaining that the point of this game is to get people to expand on whatever their partner says. The first rule of improv is "Yes, and . . . ", so that is what will be practiced here. Give students different topics that they will then make statements about. Their job is to answer your questions about their specified topic with, "yes, and . . . ", then expand on what you said. Start by introducing them to the audience and picking the topic they are experts in (e.g., animals, foods, vehicles, countries, sports, etc.). Ensure you make it something they are NOT really an expert in. You might start like, "ladies and gentlemen, we have here the world's leading expert on koalas. I heard you studied the koalas for over ten years." Then see where the conversation goes and expand on whatever they give to you. Spend a little bit of time with each person on stage in front of everyone, if possible. YOU ARE THE INTERVIEWER.	You on stage with one person at a time. Each interview should be 1–2 minutes Total game time: 10–20 minutes for a class size of 10	This activity is all about expanding on the conversation in a way that is still relatively on topic. In the shoelace example given in the individual game plan, all those statements are possible given that person is an expert. Those occurrences are all a possibility for that person but are also all on topic. It is important to be able to have flexibility in a conversation but also be a contributor so the other person isn't doing all the talking (or listening). This game is about finding that balance and having a back-and-forth conversation.

| Closing | Take turns with students sharing something that was really fun or something that they learned. I usually go last and try to give them praise for efforts and highlight a few key things that happened this week. It is good to share that you are happy that they are all there and willing to be open to trying new things. Some of them might have felt good about class and others maybe not. End with all hands in the middle doing an "Aah-Ooh-Gah!" | Whole group; standing in a circle on stage

5 minutes | Getting them to debrief about the positive experience will keep them positive moving forward and will help them find success as improvisors. |

SAMPLE SCHEDULE: WEEK 3

GAME	EXPLANATION	FORMAT & SETUP	WHY?
Opening	Start with two deep breaths to help the class get centered and focused. I always say, "Let's take two deep breaths . . . one . . . and one more . . . that is our cue to leave everything out there, out there, and just be here." We then share the smallest positive thing that happened since you saw them last. SMALLEST thing, not a huge thing.	Whole group; standing in a circle on stage 5–10 minutes	Taking a moment to practice some positivity will help set the tone for class each week. This is also a great way to check in with each student and relax any potential tension they may have from their day. Additionally, this helps students practice communicating with each other in a safe space.
Zip Zap Zop	Students take turns pointing to each other and saying Zip, Zap, Zop. You start by pointing to someone and saying Zip, they then point to someone else and say Zap, they then point to a different person and say Zop. That repeats until someone makes a mistake, at which point everyone leans into the middle of the circle and says "Aah-Ooh-Gah!"	Whole group; standing in a circle on stage 5–10 minutes	Typically done first in a warmup. It is a chance for everyone to speak in a unified voice, to move quickly without overthinking, and to deal with failure at a very simple activity without repercussion.

GAME	EXPLANATION	FORMAT & SETUP	WHY?
Superhero (Halloween Edition)	One at a time students will get on stage and introduce their Halloween costume or a Halloween character, including a description about their costume/character. They then answer a few questions from the audience about their character. They will continue to be this character for the next game.	One person at a time on stage 10–15 minutes	Students will have to come up with an entire storyline for their character and portray that character in different scenarios. The character creation aspect of this game is critical to decision making and relationships, which you will see when you set up the scenes later on.
Brunch With . . . (Halloween Edition)	Students act out a conversation based on the Halloween characters they introduced in the previous game. Start with them working in pairs and introducing their character/costume again. Then match them with different characters. Really work on them trying to take on another person's perspective (e.g., Batman and SpongeBob are out for lunch, what do they talk about? What do they eat? etc.). Don't worry about any of the specific information that is being shared yet – just try to get them to interact with each other. (Do two rounds.)	Two people on stage at a time 15–20 minutes	When you sit down to have brunch with someone you talk about more than just the restaurant. What else would a character have concerns about? This is an opportunity to explore playing another character while maintaining a conversation, sharing insight, discussing struggles that person might face, and giving advice from that person's perspective.

GAME	EXPLANATION	FORMAT & SETUP	WHY?
	This game provides a different way of making up answers on the spot and develops confidence on stage. In *Expert*, one person answers questions about a topic they know nothing about. I'd stick to animals, places, or foods to get things going. The student answering questions is, in reality, not an expert and so answers the questions with a made-up answer. They do not need to try to be funny but should just practice responding on topic, giving details, and being confident.	One person fielding questions from audience 10–15 minutes	To build confidence, encourage rapid responses and saying the first appropriate thing that comes to mind, gain an understanding of the importance of timing of jokes (so adding to joke-telling ability), and work on "Yes, and . . ." as a concept.
Expert			
	This game is similar to *Job Interview*, but the questions come from the audience. If you are an expert on crocodiles, a question/answer might be, "Where do crocodiles live?" "They live at Balboa park."		
	Player A makes a statement about their location. Player B presents a challenge based on their location. Player A then presents the solution to the challenge. The scene does not have to be exactly three lines, but it should be short.	Two people on stage; the rest are lined up on either side 15–20 minutes	Starts to build the group-thinking mentality needed for longer/more advanced scenes, addresses "yes, and . . ." as a concept, helps with beginning scene work as it teaches students to not just say where they are but to interact with where they are, and also helps develop quick thinking.
3-Line Scene			

GAME	EXPLANATION	FORMAT & SETUP	WHY?
Emotional Sentence	One at a time, students will walk to the front center of the stage. The class would have previously suggested a simple sentence. Each student has to say the same sentence but with a different emotion behind it. The class then needs to guess what the emotion was.	One student at a time on stage 30 seconds per student	To show emotion by adjusting body posture and movements and changing vocal intonation. For the audience, they need to be able to read those cues and interpret what is being said by those body postures and gestures.
Closing	Take turns with students sharing something that was really fun or something that they learned. I usually go last and try to give them praise for efforts and highlight a few key things that happened this week. It is good to share that you are happy that they are all there and willing to be open to trying new things. Some of them might have felt good about class and others maybe not. End with all hands in the middle doing an "Aah–Ooh–Gah!"	Whole group; standing in a circle on stage 5 minutes	Getting them to debrief about the positive experience will keep them positive moving forward and will help them find success as improvisors.

SAMPLE SCHEDULE: WEEK 4

GAME	EXPLANATION	FORMAT & SETUP	WHY?
Opening	Start with two deep breaths to help the class get centered and focused. I always say, "Let's take two deep breaths . . . one . . . and one more . . . that is our cue to leave everything out there, out there, and just be here." We then share the smallest positive thing that happened since you saw them last. SMALLEST thing, not a huge thing.	Whole group; standing in a circle on stage 5–10 minutes	Taking a moment to practice some positivity will help set the tone for class each week. This is also a great way to check in with each student and relax any potential tension they may have from their day. Additionally, this helps students practice communicating with each other in a safe space.
Whoosh Bong	Students stand in a circle. One student begins by saying "Whoosh!" to their right or left. The student who the Whoosh was passed to can either continue passing the Whoosh in the same direction or they can say "Bong!," which would then reverse the direction so it goes back to the previous student. Additional variations include saying "Highway!," in which case they can pass the turn across the circle to another student that they point at, or "Ramp!," which skips a player and proceeds in the same direction to the following player.	Whole group; standing in a circle on stage 5 minutes	To get students listening to the whole group and paying attention to everything going on. Additionally, this game allows for students to make mistakes in a fun way while not having to worry about being right. This is also good for developing clear communication.

GAME	EXPLANATION	FORMAT & SETUP	WHY?
Family Tradition	One at a time, students take the stage and describe to the group a family tradition that they have, real or imaginary. After they describe the tradition, two other students then create a scene in which they act out that tradition.	One person on stage at a time; the rest sitting as an audience 10 minutes	To practice hearing information that is being shared and using it to create scenes. The scenes should be based on the information, although it doesn't have to be an exact translation.
Bus Stop	One student (or two for more advanced groups) starts by sitting on a bench on the stage, which represents a bus stop. A new student enters the scene and sits next to them. This new student has a specific characteristic about them (e.g., they're very old, they have an accent, etc.). The first student has to figure out what is different about them and then take on the same characteristics, so they become the same type of character. After about 30 seconds of conversation, have both students leave the stage (this is a modification from the traditional version of the game). Two new students then enter the bus stop, one displaying a different characteristic, and the process repeats.	Two people on stage at a time; the rest sitting in audience 15–20 minutes minutes	This game forces students to make strong, easily identifiable character choices (motivation, body postures, movements, voice, etc.). This allows for other students to do their best interpretation of that character and show those same attributes in their own way.

GAME	EXPLANATION	FORMAT & SETUP	WHY?
	Students are each assigned an animal, with there being two of each animal assigned (so two people will be assigned the same animal). Students will not know what animals other students have been assigned. Students are then spread around the room and start making sounds and performing actions that can be associated with their assigned animal. They then have to try to find their "animal partner." Try to avoid animals that make similar sounds (e.g., lions and tigers). In a group of four or five, for example, you could have two birds and two dogs, or two cats and three fish.	Small groups spread around the room 10 minutes	To show a character in multiple different ways and really understand the point of view of that character/animal. Important aspects of any character are how they think, what motivates them, and how they move in their environment. Using animals provides an easy way to practice showing those things.
Penguin	The goal is for them to walk, talk, and act like their assigned animal while also paying attention to others in the room so they can find their animal partner. REMIND them not to be too loud. An advanced version is for them to do it silently (emphasizing how they walk and pantomime).		

| Expert | This game provides a different way of making up answers on the spot and develops confidence on stage. In *Expert*, one person answers questions about a topic they know nothing about. I'd stick to animals, places, or foods to get things going. The student answering questions is, in reality, not an expert and so answers the questions with a made-up answer. They do not need to try to be funny but should just practice responding on topic, giving details, and being confident. | One person fielding questions from audience 10–15 minutes | To build confidence, encourage rapid responses and saying the first appropriate thing that comes to mind, gain an understanding of the importance of timing of jokes (so adding to joke-telling ability), and work on "Yes, and . . ." as a concept. |
| | This game is similar to *Job Interview*, but the questions come from the audience. If you are an expert on crocodiles, a question/answer might be, "Where do crocodiles live?" "They live at Balboa park." | | |

GAME	EXPLANATION	FORMAT & SETUP	WHY?
Where are you?	Students step on stage one at a time and mime being in a location. They stay on stage for approximately 30 seconds, adding detail to their location until the class guesses where they are.	One student on stage at a time About 30 seconds per student	To encourage students to slow down and show very pronounced pantomime. By interacting with the space and using it, they can give the audience and other students a clear vision of what they see. But, they have to show with some precision what they are seeing or it is left for the audience to guess (which leads to confusion and pulls away from the scene).
Closing	Take turns with students sharing something that was really fun or something that they learned. I usually go last and try to give them praise for efforts and highlight a few key things that happened this week. It is good to share that you are happy that they are all there and willing to be open to trying new things. Some of them might have felt good about class and others maybe not. End with all hands in the middle doing an "Aah-Ooh-Gah!"	Whole group; standing in a circle on stage 5 minutes	Getting them to debrief about the positive experience will keep them positive moving forward and will help them find success as improvisors.

SAMPLE SCHEDULE: WEEK 5

GAME	EXPLANATION	FORMAT & SETUP	WHY?
Opening	Start with two deep breaths to help the class get centered and focused. I always say, "Let's take two deep breaths . . . one . . . and one more . . . that is our cue to leave everything out there, out there, and just be here." We then share the smallest positive thing that happened since you saw them last. SMALLEST thing, not a huge thing.	Whole group; standing in a circle on stage 5–10 minutes	Taking a moment to practice some positivity will help set the tone for class each week. This is also a great way to check in with each student and relax any potential tension they may have from their day. Additionally, this helps students practice communicating with each other in a safe space.
Whoosh Bong	Students stand in a circle. One student begins by saying "Whoosh!" to their right or left. The student who the Whoosh was passed to can either continue passing the Whoosh in the same direction or they can say "Bong!," which would then reverse the direction so it goes back to the previous student. Additional variations include saying "Highway!," in which case they can pass the turn across the circle to another student that they point at, or "Ramp!," which skips a player and proceeds in the same direction to the following player.	Whole group; standing in a circle on stage 5 minutes	To get students listening to the whole group and paying attention to everything going on. Additionally, this game allows for students to make mistakes in a fun way while not having to worry about being right. This is also good for developing clear communication.

GAME	EXPLANATION	FORMAT & SETUP	WHY?
I Declare/Predict	Teacher gets a subject from the class. One at a time, students step on stage and make a prediction about that object. They then field questions from the class about their prediction. After 30 seconds to a minute, another student makes a different prediction about the same subject and the game continues.	One student on stage at a time 10 minutes	This game has several skills going on at the same time. First, it involves getting up on stage in front of an audience and making a statement with confidence, which can be hard to do. Second, it is about exploring various aspects of a topic so as not to repeat a previous student's response. This requires the student to think of all the ways in which you can key in on a topic, which can lead to a wider variety of scenes with more varied realities.
Superhero	Students take turns getting on stage and introducing their superhero character to the class. They can pretend to be anything they want or can be an existing character, but they have to explain it and try to show one action that this person might do. For example, if I want to be Wonder Woman, I'd explain how I'd fly my plane and then answer follow-up questions.	One person on stage at a time; the rest sitting as an audience 10 minutes	Students will have to come up with an entire storyline for their character and portray that character in different scenarios. The character creation aspect of this game is critical to decision making and relationships, which you will see when you set up the scenes later on.

GAME	EXPLANATION	FORMAT & SETUP	WHY?
Superhero Scenes	This is an expansion of the previous game where they get to pretend to be the superhero or supervillain they created. If I'm Peter Parker and you are Dr. Frost, what do we talk about?	Two people on stage at a time; the rest sitting in the audience 15–20 minutes	To create scenes that build on previous character creation.
Good/ Bad Advice	This is a quick, fun game to end class. You are on stage as a moderator or acting as host for a game show where the audience asks questions seeking advice. These questions can be about anything (e.g., How do I get out of doing homework? What should I do to get an allowance? My brother is mean, what trick can I play on him?) The player in the first chair gives good advice that people would like to hear, while the player in the second chair gives bad advice that would not be good to follow. Answer two to three questions then switch to the next group of players.	Teacher acting as host fielding questions from audience; two people on stage 10–15 minutes	To answer questions on topic and with details using a character's perspective, and strengthening students' ability to be on stage in front of an audience for longer time periods.

GAME	EXPLANATION	FORMAT & SETUP	WHY?
185	Students stand in a line against the back wall of the stage. The teacher picks a topic (e.g., profession, animal, object) and if a student comes up with a good joke/pun around that topic they step to the front center of the stage and deliver the following joke: "185 (blanks) walk into a bar. The bartender says, 'Hey, we don't serve (blanks) here.' The (blanks) reply, (punchline). This continues until the students cannot come up with a new joke, with a new topic then being chosen. You might need to explain puns and do a few practice rounds. Also, start with a suggestion of an animal then move on to occupations.	Whole group lined up on stage 10–15 minutes	To build confidence and deliver an on-topic joke with good timing and with confidence. Also, to find creative puns and jokes from normal everyday items, become more comfortable with risk taking (i.e., standing in front of an audience and delivering jokes), and overcome failure (i.e., have the opportunity to tell another joke if one didn't go well).

GAME	EXPLANATION	FORMAT & SETUP	WHY?
Closing	Take turns with students sharing something that was really fun or something that they learned. I usually go last and try to give them praise for efforts and highlight a few key things that happened this week. It is good to share that you are happy that they are all there and willing to be open to trying new things. Some of them might have felt good about class and others maybe not. End with all hands in the middle doing an "Aah-Ooh-Gah!"	Whole group; standing in a circle on stage 5 minutes	Getting them to debrief about the positive experience will keep them positive moving forward and will help them find success as improvisors.

SAMPLE SCHEDULE: WEEK 6

GAME	EXPLANATION	FORMAT & SETUP	WHY?
Opening	Start with two deep breaths to help the class get centered and focused. I always say, "Let's take two deep breaths . . . one . . . and one more . . . that is our cue to leave everything out there, out there, and just be here." We then share the smallest positive thing that happened since you saw them last. SMALLEST thing, not a huge thing.	Whole group; standing in a circle on stage 5–10 minutes	Taking a moment to practice some positivity will help set the tone for class each week. This is also a great way to check in with each student and relax any potential tension they may have from their day. Additionally, this helps students practice communicating with each other in a safe space.
Whoosh Bong	Students stand in a circle. One student begins by saying "Whoosh!" to their right or left. The student who the Whoosh was passed to can either continue passing the Whoosh in the same direction or they can say "Bong!," which would then reverse the direction so it goes back to the previous student. Additional variations include saying "Highway!," in which case they can pass the turn across the circle to another student that they point at, or "Ramp!," which skips a player and proceeds in the same direction to the following player.	Whole group; standing in a circle on stage 5 minutes	To get students listening to the whole group and paying attention to everything going on. Additionally, this game allows for students to make mistakes in a fun way while not having to worry about being right. This is also good for developing clear communication.

GAME	EXPLANATION	FORMAT & SETUP	WHY?
I Feel/ You Feel	Two students start on stage. Each is given a different emotion. They are given a single location and then play out a short scene in that location while feeling their emotion. The scene, and emotion played, can be about where they are, who they're with, or what their circumstances are.	Two students on stage together in a short scene 2–3 minutes per group	To develop students' ability to read and show emotions in various ways. The audience wants to see how students portray emotions by what they say, how they say it, and how they interact with the environment. By giving them an emotion that drives all of their decisions, students can use that to shape their character.
Where Are You?	Students step on stage one at a time and mime being in a location. They stay on stage for approximately 30 seconds, adding detail to their location until the class guesses where they are.	One student at a time on stage About 30 seconds per student	To encourage students to slow down and show very pronounced pantomime. By interacting with the space and using it, they can give the audience and other students a clear vision of what they see. But, they have to show with some precision what they are seeing or it is left for the audience to guess (which leads to confusion and pulls away from the scene).

GAME	EXPLANATION	FORMAT & SETUP	WHY?
Blind Freeze	Two students on stage randomly move about for a few seconds until the teacher yells "Freeze!" They freeze in position for a moment and then unfreeze and begin a scene that justifies why they were in that position. After a few beats (perhaps 15 seconds or so), the teacher again calls out "Freeze" and two new students come in and take the exact position that the original students are now in, beginning a new scene from there.	Two people on stage; the rest lined up on either side 15–20 minutes	By using pantomime as a way to start scenes, students learn more about how to show their environment to the audience. This also teaches students to use the entirety of the space they are creating. This helps bring scenes to life and helps students use more of their abstract thinking skills.
Categories	Students stand shoulder to shoulder facing the audience. The teacher gets a general category (i.e., "desserts") from the audience. When pointed to, students need to say one thing that fits the category. The teacher kneels or stands in front of students and points to them randomly.	Approx. six to eight students standing across the stage facing the audience 5–10 minutes	To build confidence, practice listening to others on stage, practice stage presence, develop quick thinking skills, encourage students to say something and not freeze when put on the spot.

GAME	EXPLANATION	FORMAT & SETUP	WHY?
185	Students stand in a line against the back wall of the stage. The teacher picks a topic (e.g., profession, animal, object) and if a student comes up with a good joke/pun around that topic they step to the front center of the stage and deliver the following joke: "185 (blanks) walk into a bar. The bartender says, 'Hey, we don't serve (blanks) here.' The (blanks) reply, (punchline). This continues until the students cannot come up with a new joke, with a new topic then being chosen. You might need to explain puns and do a few practice rounds. Also, start with a suggestion of an animal then move on to occupations.	Whole group lined up on stage 10–15 minutes	To build confidence and deliver an on-topic joke with good timing and with confidence. Also, to find creative puns and jokes from normal everyday items, become more comfortable with risk taking (i.e., standing in front of an audience and delivering jokes), and overcome failure (i.e., have the opportunity to tell another joke if one didn't go well).
Closing	Take turns with students sharing something that was really fun or something that they learned. I usually go last and try to give them praise for efforts and highlight a few key things that happened this week. It is good to share that you are happy that they are all there and willing to be open to trying new things. Some of them might have felt good about class and others maybe not. End with all hands in the middle doing an "Aah-Ooh-Gah!"	Whole group; standing in a circle on stage 5 minutes	Getting them to debrief about the positive experience will keep them positive moving forward and will help them find success as improvisors.

WEEK 1	WEEK 2	WEEK 3	WEEK 4	WEEK 5	WEEK 6
Opening	Opening	Opening	Opening	Opening	Opening
Name Game	Name Game	Zip	Whoosh Bong	Whoosh Bong	Whoosh Bong
Zip	GO	Superhero	Family Tradition	I Declare	I Feel / You Feel
Yes, and...	Zip	Brunch with	Bus Stop	Superhero	Where are you?
Story	Animal Clue	Expert	Penguin	Superhero Scenes	Blind Freeze
Good Advice	Story	3 Line Scene	Expert	Good Advice	Categories
Closing	Yes, and...	Emotional Sentence	Where are you?	185	185
	Closing	Closing	Closing	Closing	Closing

GAME TYPE

Warmup
Character
Scenework/Story
Quick Thinking
Emotion
Pantomime

CHAPTER 5

TERMINOLOGY

Aah-Ooh-Gah!	The sound made by an old-time car horn. The group all says the word out loud when they make an error during a warmup game to clear the slate.
Blocking	Rejecting or ignoring another actor's idea or offer during a scene. This usually results in the scene stagnating or not moving forward.
Conflict	The concept of having a goal that is being thwarted by either another character's goal or an internal or external situation. Overcoming the conflict provides the dramatic/comedic narrative in storytelling.
Creating a "where"	Developing the location for a scene on stage. This can be done through behavior or dialogue, or both.
Cut to	During a scene, switching the action to a new location. This can be done by either wiping the scene or by directly telling the audience (e.g., "Cut to the principal's office").
Denial	Rejecting the idea or offer of another performer on stage. Interchangeable with *blocking*.
Environment	The location or setting where a scene takes place.
Gibberish	A nonsensical language. Similar to how the Minions might sound.

DOI: 10.4324/9781003207627-5

Justifying	Clarifying an offer so that it makes sense within the context of a scene. A character might justify leaving a scene by explaining why they are leaving or where they are going, for example.
Mime/Pantomime	Dealing with objects that are not actually there in a realistic way.
Narrative	The idea of creating and telling a story. The narrative is the plotline.
Objective	The main "want" of a character. What it is that the character is really after.
Offer	A line or action directed to another actor that sets up some kind of response and is designed to move the scene forward.
Stage Left/Stage Right	The directional point of view from the actor's perspective. If an actor is on stage, then Stage Left refers to their left, not the audience's.
Stage Wipe	The act of switching a scene to a new location by crossing in front of the actors and starting a new scene in the new location as the other actors exit.
Status	Refers to where a character appears in a pecking order. For example, a principal is higher status than a student. This can change based on circumstances and is the basis for numerous types of stories.
Stay in the Realm	Keeping ideas all within the same overall universe. Useful to mention, for example, if an actor adds fantasy to a realistic scene or brings in completely unrelated ideas that will confuse the scene.
Suggestion	An idea that is received from the audience to begin a scene.
Theory of Mind	The ability to attribute mental states to oneself and others – to understand that others may have different feelings than your own.
Upstage/Downstage	Upstage is the back of the stage (farthest from the audience). Downstage is towards the front of the stage.
Yes, and . . .	The basic concept of improv. It means to agree to a partner's idea and then add information to it.

INDEX

Printed in Australia
AUHW011531210223
374834AU00019B/138

9 781032 075501